The Philosophy of Miracles

The Philosophy of Miracles

David Corner

continuum

Continuum
The Tower Building, 11 York Road, London SE1 7NX
80 Maiden Lane, Suite 704, New York NY 10038

British Library Cataloguing-in-Publication Data
A catalogue record for this book is available from the British Library.

ISBN: HB: 0-8264-8887-0
ISBN-13: HB: 978-08264-8887-9

Library of Congress Cataloguing-in-Publication Data

Corner, David.
  The philosophy of miracles / by David Corner.
     p. cm.
  Includes bibliographical references.
  ISBN 0–8264–8887–0
1.   Miracles. 2. Philosophical theology.   I. Title.
  BT97.C72 2007
  212- -dc22

                                                          2006020210

Typeset by Kenneth Burnley, Wirral, Cheshire
Printed and bound in Great Britain by Biddles Ltd, King's Lynn, Norfolk

To Merv Corner and Jean Parker

Contents

Acknowledgements   ix

Introduction   1
Conceptions of the Miraculous   6
  Supernaturalistic Conceptions of the Miraculous   6
  Teleology and the Miraculous   10
  Contextual Criteria for the Miraculous   11

1 Miracles and the Laws of Nature   17
The Logical Impossibility of a Violation   18
Violations as Nonrepeatable Counterinstances to
    Natural Law   22
  Objection 1: Nonrepeatable Counterinstances as
    Falsifying a Law   24
  Objection 2: Identifying Nonrepeatable Counterinstances   25
  Objection 3: Counterinstance as Anomaly   28
A Supernaturalistic Conception of Natural Law   30
  Identifying Supernatural Intrusions: An Objection   32
  Supernatural Intrusions: Lost Contrast   35
  A Supernaturalistic Response   38

2 Miracles and Causes   40
What is a Supernatural Cause?   42
Nature as Causally Open   44
  Trans-domain Laws   48
Dualism and the Supernatural   49

viii   *Contents*

3 Supernatural Explanation   53

Nowell-Smith and Predictive Expansion   55
Do Explanations Always Rely on Laws?   63
Paul Dietl's Response to Nowell-Smith's Challenge   67
  Analysis of Dietl's Response   69
  Problems with Dietl's Response   70
Divine Agency in Religious Practice   74

4 Miracle as Basic Action   79

Must 'Miracle' Be Conceived Teleologically?   82
Divine Agency Without Supernatural Causation   83
Miracles and Interaction   88
Miracles and Natural Causes   90
Miracle, Mystery, and the God-of-the-gaps   91

5 Miracle and Divine Agency   94

The World as God's Body   95
  Basic Mental Acts   98
  Psychokinesis as Basic Act   98
Non-Basic Divine Agency   101
  Divine Agency and Non-determined Processes   102
The Causal Joint   105
Locating Divine Basic Actions: How Far Down Should We Go?   109
  Divine Manipulation of Microprocesses: An Alternative 113
  Arguments for Divine Basic Actions at the Macro Level 115
Quantum Gaps and Special Divine Agency   119

6 A Context for Miracles   127

Thankability and the Miraculous   130
  Thankability and the Subjective: An Objection   135
  Due Thankability   136
  Due Thankability and Apologetic   136
Miracle, Coincidence, and Counterfactual   139
  Counterfactuals and Basic Actions   142

Notes   147
Bibliography   156
Index   159

Acknowledgements

I owe thanks to several people for their help on this project, which builds upon material written in pursuit of a PhD at the University of California, Santa Barbara. I am very grateful to William Forgie for detailed comments on earlier incarnations of this manuscript. I am indebted as well to Matthew Hanser and Thomas Holden for their insight. I also owe much to comments on the initial draft that were made by D. Z. Phillips. Prof. Phillips has greatly influenced my thinking on this topic, in conversation as well as by his published work. Joseph Lynch also provided me with fruitful discussion of many of the issues that emerge here. None of these philosophers is responsible for any errors that remain, particularly given that the current version includes material on which they have not had the opportunity to comment.

I thank my family for their support, and for enduring the hardships that this project brought with it: my wife Lesslie, my son Jordan, and my daughters, Samantha and Gwen. Finally, I dedicate this book to my parents, who brought me to this place, and who nurtured my siblings and me in an environment in which creative activity was part of everyday life.

Introduction

It has been common for some time to think of a miracle as a natural event possessing a supernatural cause. Such a supernaturalistic account of miracles might be constructed with an eye to apologetic concerns, with the hope that the occurrence of a miracle might provide a defense for theism. The general strategy of such an apologetic appeal is to suggest that a miracle is an event that nature could not produce on its own. It is thought of as an event that is incapable of receiving a natural explanation. Thus the supernaturalist hopes that the occurrence of a miracle will point to the operation of a causal force from outside of nature, i.e. one that is supernatural.

My concern in this book will be to show the liabilities of such an account of miracles, and to show how our concept of the miraculous may do without it. In its stead I will offer a *non-causal* account of miracles. My motivation, expressed in the broadest possible terms, is to rescue the concept of 'miracle' from the quasi-scientific language of the supernaturalist, and to show that the best understanding of a miracle is not one that tries to place it in relation to scientific notions such as that of a law of nature; it is one that understands a miracle to be an extraordinary expression of divine agency – where this need not be understood in terms of divine *causality* – and as an event that has a role to play within theistic religious practice.

I should make clear that it is not my intention here to rule out the possibility that we can meaningfully speak of miracles as being, in some sense, supernatural – though I will not attempt to defend this suggestion here. Rather, in my references to supernaturalism, in what follows, I wish to be understood as talking about what might be called '*causal* supernaturalism'. Such a position attempts to construe supernatural activity in terms that closely parallel the way we speak of physical causes, as, for example, supernatural *forces* or *influences* that might override, or take the place of, *physical* forces and influences.

In my first three chapters I hope to show the problems faced by such a supernaturalistic conception of 'miracle'. Quite often, when the supernaturalist wants to say that a miracle is an event that nature could not produce on its own, she will attempt to defend the conception of a miracle as a violation of the laws of nature, or some cognate such as a transgression, intervention and so forth. In Chapter 1, I will examine the notion of a violation. The conception of a violation is the conception of an event that somehow rends the fabric of nature, and as such is thought to be made possible only by forces operating from outside of nature. Some critics, such as Antony Flew and Alasdair McKinnon, have argued that the concept of a violation is self-contradictory. I will argue that there is no incoherence involved in saying that an event has occurred which cannot be subsumed under the laws of nature, where these laws are understood as fully determined regularities.[1] I do not, however, see why such an event should be thought of as a violation – as somehow inconsistent with the real structure of nature, or as requiring us to acknowledge the existence of anything transcending nature.

In Chapter 2, I will examine the conception of a miracle as having a *supernatural cause*. The supernaturalist tries to understand a supernatural cause as analogous to a *natural* cause. I will argue, however, that this analogy is empty. If there are such things as supernatural causes, then to the extent that we conceive of them as similar to natural causes we conceive them *as* natural; to the extent that they differ from natural causes, we can form no conception of them at all. Furthermore, to the extent that we attempt to understand supernatural entities and forces as radically different from those we find in nature, it becomes increasingly more difficult to understand how they might *interact* with natural objects. Indeed the notion of a supernatural cause brings with it problems similar to that encountered by the substance dualist in trying to account for mind–body interaction.

In Chapter 3, I will discuss the conception of a supernatural explanation. If the conception of a supernatural explanation is taken as closely parallel to the notion of a natural one, as that employed by the natural sciences, then such explanations must be testable. However, any purported supernatural explanation that satisfies this criterion will be one that fails to qualify as supernatural. I will also argue that we may conceive of an event as being miraculous, and expressing divine agency, where this is *not* a matter of explaining the event; at least, if we are held to be explaining it, the sort of explanation we are giving is markedly different from the kind of explanation provided by the natural sciences.

In Chapter 4, I hope to develop a non-causal conception of the miraculous by defending the concept of a miracle as a *basic action* on the part of God. For most human beings on most occasions, the raising of an arm is a basic action, which means that there is nothing we do to cause our arm to go up. This means that we may speak of an agent performing an action without being committed to any *causal* analysis of what she has done; raising an arm is normally something that an agent 'just does', without having to do anything else to bring it about. We do not typically think of an agent exerting any sort of force or influence upon her body in order to make her arm rise. Analogously, if we think of miracles as basic divine actions, we do not have to think of a miracle as coming about through the operation of some kind of occult force.

Speaking of miracles as divine basic actions has a very important consequence. When we describe a miracle as a divine basic action, we are making no assertion about its cause, and this means that we do not have to rule out the possibility that it might have a natural cause, or to show that its occurrence is a disruption in the fabric of nature.

In Chapter 5, I will consider two objections that may be made to my account of basic divine agency. First, I will consider a disanalogy between human and divine basic actions, which is that human basic actions are expressed in bodily movements. Divine basic actions are not so expressed, unless we wish to say that the physical universe is the body of God. I will argue that an account of miracles as basic divine actions does not require us to say that the universe is the body of God.

I will then consider the suggestion that any satisfactory account of divine agency must make clear the *causal means* by which God acts. My discussion on this point will give me a chance to say something about the implications of my account for what has come to be known as the Problem of the Causal Joint. I will try to show that if we think of miracles as basic actions on the part of God, we may speak of God as acting directly at the level of ordinary experience, without having to place the primary locus of divine action in the 'gaps' that are present in some form of non-deterministic natural process.

Finally, in Chapter 6, I will consider what sort of criteria may be employed, within the context of theistic religion, in the identification of an event as a miracle. The emphasis will be, of course, on criteria that do not require any reference to supernatural causation. There I will defend *thankability* as a sufficient condition for divine agency; that is, if any event should occur for which God is properly thankable, that event will constitute an instance of divine agency. My argument in this chapter owes much to R. F. Holland's discussion of contingency, or *coincidence*, miracles, and to the further development of the thankability criterion that is due to J. Kellenberger. I do not agree with Kellenberger that thankability is a sufficient condition for the miraculous, since God may be thankable for events that are not in any way extraordinary, and an event, to be a miracle, must be extraordinary. However, the occurrence of an extraordinary event for which thanks are due to God will qualify as a miracle.

Thankability is, I will argue, only one example of how, within the context and assumptions of theistic religious practice, we might identify an event as an instance of divine agency. What is important about the thankability criterion is that it acknowledges the religious significance of a miracle, and places it into its proper relation to theistic religious practice.

A critic may object that a miracle must be something that would not have happened had God not willed it, and that, if an event is one that can be accounted for as occurring as a result of natural causes, any reference to God's will becomes redundant. I will conclude Chapter 6 with an argument that we may conceive a miracle as something that expresses divine purpose – something that would not have occurred had God not willed for it to occur – *even though* it has a natural cause.

I should make it clear that I do not intend for the conception of 'miracle' that I offer here to have any value in religious apologetic. I am concerned to describe how one may speak of miracles within the context of a religious practice, where the reality of God is not in question. I have no interest in defending any conception of the miraculous which might, for example, be employed in an effort to persuade a religious skeptic.

With this in mind, I should point out that I will occasionally speak in terms of what is necessary for us to identify an event as a miracle, or to recognize it as miraculous. One might argue that the words 'identify' and 'recognize', used in this way, are success words; that is, that one cannot identify an event as a miracle, or recognize it as one, unless it *really is* a miracle. I could preface all of my claims about the possibility of identifying an event as a miracle by saying something like: 'Assuming that miracles occur, we may recognize them in accordance with criteria *xyz*.' But this is cumbersome. Thus, my entire book should be understood as written within the context of this hypothesis, that is, under the assumption that miracles really do occur and that we are capable in principle of distinguishing them from non-miraculous events. And once again I do not think this is unseemly given that I am concerned to speak of miracles as a practitioner of theistic religion would be expected to speak of them, that is, without supposing their occurrence to be problematic, given that I do not intend to write from the position of an apologist who seeks to provide a justification for theistic religious practice.

This is not to sweep under the carpet the serious philosophical problems associated with the claim that miracles really do occur, and that we can be justified in believing that they occur. Concern with these problems usually focuses on David Hume's skepticism about these matters. It is not my intention to address this kind of skepticism here – at least not directly – though no doubt some of what I will say here is relevant to that discussion. In any case I will alert my readers to what may seem a rather surprising fact, which is

that this is a work on miracles that contains relatively little reference to Hume, and little explicit reference to the problems associated with our having good reason to believe that a miracle has
occurred, if we cannot take for granted the reality of God and the
possibility of God's acting in the natural world.

Conceptions of the Miraculous

It will be helpful to consider some competing conceptions of the
miraculous. There appear to be common elements among various
conceptions of the miraculous that will be of interest to us. Let me
introduce some terminology that will help us to compare and
contrast these conceptions. The terms I wish to introduce revolve
around several key questions regarding the nature of a miracle. In
what follows I will speak of *supernaturalistic* conceptions of the
miraculous, as well as of *teleological* and *contextual* notions. I should
make it clear that I do not conceive these to be mutually exclusive
terms; that is, an account of miracles might be supernaturalistic and
at the same time be both teleological and contextual, though of
course another account might lack one or the other of these two
attributes.

Supernaturalistic Conceptions of the Miraculous

The first question we might ask about the concept of a miracle is:
Must a miracle be conceived as a supernaturally caused event? Many
writers insist that it must. Quite commonly[2] such a view of miracles
conceives them to be violations of natural law; for various rather
nuanced reasons, some writers prefer terms with similar import,
such as 'transgression', 'suspension', 'intervention', etc., though one
might argue that an event may be supernaturally caused *without*
its violating any natural law. Whether or not it is a violation, the
important point is that it is seen as an event that cannot be
produced by natural forces alone.

It will be helpful to say a few words about what is meant by the
term 'supernatural' here, and by the general view that depends on
reference to the supernatural, namely *supernaturalism*. It may be

easiest to understand supernaturalism in contrast to naturalism, which has two forms. *Methodological naturalism* is the view that all adequate explanations are ultimately *scientific* explanations, subsumable under the methods of the natural sciences. *Ontological* naturalism holds that the only objects that exist are natural objects, i.e. objects of the sort that may play a role in scientific explanations. By contrast, then, supernaturalism, if it is to reject both of these forms of naturalism, is the view that the natural sciences do not reveal the totality of all that there is; some phenomena cannot be explained by reference to the methods of the natural sciences, and so require supernatural explanation. Supernatural explanations will thus make reference to entities, such as God, that are of an entirely different sort from the kind of entities to which natural explanations refer.

Naturalism is sometimes characterized as holding that nature is uniform, which is to say that all events in nature conform to laws which can be verified by means of observation. Naturalists do commonly hold this view – confidence in the uniformity of nature is an important part of the scientific enterprise – but strictly speaking this represents an additional metaphysical commitment regarding the nature of the universe and its susceptibility to human understanding. One does not have to reject naturalism to admit that nature does not conform to deterministic laws, and this fact will be quite significant for our purposes here. A failure of uniformity, or what a supernaturalist might refer to as a violation of natural law, would thus signify to the naturalist only that there are limits to our ability to understand and predict natural phenomena – i.e. to *explain* them.

It is important to recognize that when the supernaturalist speaks of an event as having a supernatural cause, she means for the notion of a supernatural cause to be sufficiently analogous to that of a natural cause so that an event's having a natural cause, sufficient to bring it about, will exclude the possibility of its having one that is supernatural. If a purported miracle is found to have such a natural cause, this means that there is no reason to go looking for one that is supernatural. But it is hard to say just *how* they are to be understood as analogous given their obvious difference – i.e. that the one is a natural cause, operating in space and time, and the other is not. (I will have more to say about this difficulty in Chapter 2.) We may be forgiven for suspecting that the notion of a supernatural cause is fundamentally confused.

One possibility is to think of supernatural causation as being an instance of *event* causation; we do not normally admit the existence of two distinct events as causes for some phenomenon, where each would be sufficient to explain that phenomenon. Thus if the eight-ball rolls into the corner pocket of a billiard table, saying that Betty knocked it in by striking it with the cue ball would normally count against the applicability of any other explanation for how it got there, e.g. that it was blown in by a strong gust of wind or that it rolled in when Fred lifted up the other end of the table. In such a case, to propose that there is an additional (event-) causal factor operating is to propose a redundancy of causes. Now if the cue ball rolls into the pocket and we cannot find a natural cause that was responsible for pushing it in, we must, on the supernaturalist view of things, suppose that the push was provided by something supernatural.

The alternative would be to take seriously the proposition that there *was* no cause for the ball's rolling into the pocket. This is something that the supernaturalist will resist. The supernaturalist typically supposes that if a putative miracle has no natural cause, this is enough to establish that it has a cause that is supernatural. As I hope to show in Chapter 2, however, we do not seem to have good reasons for preferring to say that an event has a supernatural cause over saying that it has no cause at all.

One could speak of supernatural causes differently. One model would be something perhaps roughly analogous to the Aristotelian view, according to which there may be more than one kind of cause operating when the ball falls into the corner pocket. Thus one might adduce a *final* (or teleological) cause for the event – I intended for the ball to go into the corner pocket – that can coexist peacefully with a natural cause (e.g. it was struck by the eight-ball). The supernaturalist does commonly want to associate supernatural causes with divine intentions; however, supernaturalism, as I wish to understand it here, understands supernatural causation as a rival hypothesis to the suggestion that a natural cause is operating. Supernatural causes are thought to operate only in the gaps that are left by natural causes; finding a natural cause for an event renders any reference to a supernatural cause redundant.

Perhaps the earliest attempt to conceive of miracles as having a supernatural cause is that of St. Thomas Aquinas, who held, in *Summa Contra Gentiles* III: 101, that a miracle is something done 'by divine power outside of the usual established order of events'. He explicitly denies that any being save God can work a miracle, since 'what is entirely subject to established order cannot work beyond that order' (*Summa Contra Gentiles* III: 102), though he insisted that a miracle is not contrary to nature, since it is in the nature of all created things to be susceptible to God's will (*Summa Contra Gentiles* III: 100). On Aquinas's view there is an order in nature by which events normally transpire, and this order is abrogated on occasion in the production, by God, of a miracle. Thus the occurrence of a miracle requires the operation of a force that is external to nature, i.e. one that is supernatural. It cannot be explained by reference to natural forces alone.

C. S. Lewis has argued that a miracle is an event which cannot be explained except by reference to the supernatural. He defines a miracle as 'an interference with Nature by supernatural power' (1947: 5) and tells us that 'a miracle is emphatically not an event without cause' (1947: 60); it is only that it lacks any *natural* cause. On his view people object to miracles because 'they start by taking nature to be the whole of reality', but 'they have mistaken a partial system within reality, namely Nature, for the whole' (1947: 60). It is clear that Lewis thinks that the occurrence of a miracle has apologetic value; that is, it requires, for its explanation, an appeal to a reality *beyond* nature.

More recently, Robert Larmer has offered a definition for 'miracle' that is supernaturalistic; it is, on his view, a necessary condition for an event's being a miracle that it is beyond the power of nature to produce (1996: 14). Larmer also thinks that the occurrence of such an event may have apologetic value for Christian theism, arguing that 'if an event can be satisfactorily explained by theism as being a miracle, but physicalism can offer no satisfactory explanation of it, then we are justified in seeing it as evidence for the superiority of theism over physicalism' (1996: 114).

Teleology and the Miraculous

A second question we might ask is, *Must a miracle express divine agency?* Anyone who answers 'yes' to this question holds what I will refer to as a *teleological* conception of the miraculous, where 'teleological' means only that a miracle must be an action, or express agency. Some commentators have denied the necessity of such a criterion for the miraculous, thus embracing a non-teleological conception of 'miracle'. The simplest way to do this is to suppose that it is a sufficient condition for an event's being a miracle that it have a supernatural cause. Thus consider as an example the movement of a glacier, which might etch lines in a wall of rock; we can account for this by reference to purely mechanical forces, without reference to the intentions of any agent. One might argue that similar lines might appear without any natural cause being involved; there might be some supernatural force analogous to the sort of force that may be exerted by a glacier – at least in its effects – which does not involve the intentions of any agent such as God.

It is possible that David Hume intends to provide a non-teleological definition of 'miracle' when he tells us that a miracle is 'a violation of the laws of nature' (1975: 114), omitting, at least at first, any reference to divine agency. However, Hume's case is not so clear, since he immediately follows this first description of a miracle with another that includes a teleological criterion, saying that 'a miracle may be accurately defined, as a transgression of a law of nature by a particular volition of the Deity, or by the interposition of some invisible agent' (1975: 115n). What is odd about his offering this teleological conception of 'miracle' is that he makes no use of it. It is possible that he intends to *define* 'miracle' teleologically, but that the teleological element is simply not relevant to his critique; what makes it irrational to accept testimony for the miraculous has nothing to do with a miracle's expressing divine agency. The problem as Hume sees it is that, as a necessary condition, such testimony reports an event that is inconsistent with natural law.

A clearer example of a non-teleological definition for 'miracle' is provided by Stephen Mumford, who has recently defended a purely causal conception of the miraculous that omits any reference to divine agency, suggesting that any natural event with a supernatural cause will qualify (2001). Mumford's account has been criticized by Steve Clarke as failing to capture a properly religious sense of the notion; as Clarke argues, 'miracles are usually thought to be acts that have religious significance. They have religious significance because they are instrumental to the plans of supernatural agents' (2003: 460). Thus Clarke wants to defend a teleological conception of the miraculous.

Contextual Criteria for the Miraculous

A third question one might ask is: *Does the context in which an event occurs play a role in whether it is to be considered a miracle?* No doubt there are many possible contexts that might be thought relevant to whether an event ought to be conceived as a miracle. One way of making this out would be to say that an event will qualify as a miracle only if it has the right kind of relationship to the interests of human beings. Another might be to say that it must be possible to incorporate the event into a religious view of the world, or into a religious practice. One might also wish to say that an event does not constitute a miracle unless it is capable of evoking a particular sort of response on the part of humans or other sentient creatures.[3]

The possibility of associating a miracle with a particular response on the part of human beings is in keeping with the etymological origin of the word 'miracle', which is from the Latin *miraculum*, derived from the verb *mirari*, to wonder; thus the most general characterization of a miracle is as an event that provokes wonder. Of course the property of eliciting wonder in human beings cannot be a sufficient condition for the miraculous, since many things might provoke wonder that are not miracles; we might wonder how an Olympic athlete can lift a 473-pound dumbbell over his head, but his lifting it would not normally be considered miraculous. Nevertheless it might be held to be a necessary condition for the miraculous.

Wittgenstein offers what seems to be a contextual view of

miracles, given his emphasis on their symbolic significance. In *Culture and Value* he writes:

> A miracle is, as it were, a gesture that God makes. As a man sits quietly and then makes an impressive gesture, God lets the world run on smoothly and then accompanies the words of a saint by a symbolic occurrence, a gesture of nature. It would be an instance if, when a saint has spoken, the trees around him bowed, as if in reverence. (1980: 45e)

A miracle cannot, it would seem, possess the kind of symbolic significance that a gesture may enjoy without its occurring in a context in which it can be *interpreted* as having that significance.

A contextual approach is also common among philosophers who are influenced by Wittgenstein. Thus Peter Winch has recently taken up Wittgenstein's description of a miracle as a gesture. Winch notes that a gesture typically has its significance only within a cultural context. For example, someone's bending at the waist can be recognized as a bow only by reference to a culturally based convention by which bending at the waist may be understood as a gesture of respect or deference. Our recognition of the character of such a gesture is expressed by a particular kind of response, for example, bowing in return. Winch writes:

> Something similar holds in the case of miracles, too. An event, however astounding, can be called a miracle only in a context which contains the possibility, however conditioned, of someone's reacting to it in the way characteristic of reaction to a miracle. (1995: 211)

Winch wants to argue that an important part of the characteristic response to a miracle is a willingness to desist from looking for an explanation for the event. One reacts instead with wonder or praise.

R. F. Holland also gives us a contextual conception of the miraculous – one which I will defend in my final chapter. He agrees that a miracle may confound our understanding of what is physically possible, but denies that this is a necessary component of the concept of 'miracle'. On the contrary, a religiously significant coincidence may be miraculous on his view. What gives such coincidences their significance is 'their relation to human hopes and needs and fears, their effects for good or ill upon our lives' (1965: 44). Furthermore it is important to Holland that the occurrence of a miracle be able to play a role in a religious form of life; it must be something that can be prayed for or made the subject of a vow, 'all of which can only take place against the background of a religious tradition' (1965: 44).

Finally, John Hick has argued for a conception of religious faith as a form of 'experiencing-as'. Inspired by Wittgenstein's discussion of seeing-as in the *Philosophical Investigations* (194e), Hick has argued that while the theist and the atheist live in the same physical environment, they experience it differently; the theist sees a significance in the events of her life that prompts her to describe her experience as a continuing interaction with God (1973: ch. 2). A theist, for example, might benefit from an unexpected job opportunity and experience this as an expression of divine providence, whereas an atheist would not view it in this way. The apprehension of a miracle by a religious believer is an extension of this. Regarding miracles in particular, Hick (1973: 51) writes:

A miracle, whatever else it may be, is an event through which we become vividly and immediately conscious of God as acting towards us. A startling happening, even if it should involve a suspension of natural law, does not constitute for us a miracle in the religious sense of the word if it fails to make us intensely aware of God's presence. In order to be miraculous, an event must be experienced as religiously significant.

It is, on Hick's view, a necessary condition of an event's being a miracle that it *affect* us in a certain way, bringing us to an awareness of the presence of God. Thus he explicitly makes the question of whether an event is a miracle depending, at least in part, on what the observer makes of it; if a violation occurred in the forest (so to speak) and there were no one present to witness it, and so to become intensely aware of God's presence through it, it would not be a miracle on his view.

We should note a connection between a teleological conception of 'miracle' and one that is contextual. We are hardly likely to suppose that an event expresses divine agency unless we are able to see it as relevant to the human condition. God does not merely act; within the domain of theistic religion, God's actions are largely directed *toward us*. I do not see any way to rule out the possibility that the lifting of a stone on an uninhabited planetoid might be an expression of divine agency, but it would be hard for us to understand such an event as fulfilling any divine purpose. Similarly we are unlikely to suppose that God is involved in any occurrence that cannot be made relevant to theistic religion. Thus I would not argue for any hard distinction between teleological and contextual accounts of the miraculous.

Now that I have introduced some of the criteria that various thinkers have offered for the miraculous, I can make my own intentions clear. I will begin by arguing against supernaturalistic accounts of the miraculous. I cannot, of course, address each of the major attempts to defend such an account individually, but I do hope to point out some of the liabilities common to them. After doing this, I will try to articulate a conception of the miraculous that is both teleological and contextual. It is not my intention here to offer any definition of 'miracle' that will be immune to counterexample; I am not certain such a thing can be done.[4] Rather, I am more concerned with making a negative point – one about what should *not* be included in any such definition – and that is a reference to supernatural causes. Nevertheless it may serve the purpose of clarity to give a working definition of 'miracle', since in what I have said already, I have already taken up a general commitment. A miracle is, it seems to me, an extraordinary event – and by this I mean one that contradicts any reasonable expectation we might have about what was going to happen.[5]

Some question could arise as to just what it is that makes a miracle extraordinary. People vary in their ability to predict what will happen, depending on what they know of the world. One possibility is to make the extraordinariness criterion an *epistemic* one, and say that it is enough that someone simply be unable to predict what will happen given their understanding of the conditions prior to the occurrence of a putative miracle, and their understanding of the laws of nature. A critic might object that this makes the matter of whether something constitutes a miracle a rather subjective affair. I am not too concerned about this implication, as long as we realize that given the criteria I offer here, this does not affect the question of whether it may be attributed to divine agency. I am not overly troubled by the possibility that one and the same divine action may be a miracle (or a *wonder*) relative to one person, but not to another. Indeed this may be expected if the notion of a miracle has implications in regard to the kind of response that human beings might make to it, or if it is part of the concept of a miracle that miracles must be understood as occurring in the context of a relationship between God and humanity. What is important, it seems to me, is that the criteria for *divine agency* be objective. Whether God is acting in a particular case cannot depend on how an audience views the matter.

An analogy is possible here. Suppose I give a present to a child on her birthday. I may wish, for any number of reasons, to surprise her with my gift. Naturally whether she is surprised will depend on what she knows; has she seen the unwrapped gift in my bedroom closet? But whether I am acting in relation to her, by giving her the gift, does not depend on whether she is surprised by it.

I do think it is possible to suggest objective criteria for extraordinariness, and it is important to note that this need not involve saying that a miracle must be a violation of natural law. A good number of events are, objectively speaking, *unlikely* to occur and so would justifiably surprise anyone, regardless of what they know about the world. Thus, for example, it could turn out that the parting of the Red Sea as reported in Exodus can be explained as a statistically improbable, though physically possible, result of the random movement of water molecules. Here we have a sense in which nature may be said to depart from its usual course – water, after all, does not normally part in this way – even though the event may be scientifically explicable. The fact that we can describe such a movement of water as highly unusual may justify us in calling it objectively extraordinary.

The problem with adopting such an *ontic* definition of 'extraordinary' is that it may incite a dispute over the scientific assessment of a putative miracle, to say for example just how likely the occurrence of a particular event might be. Since the concept of a miracle is an essentially religious notion, I am disinclined to accept any criterion for the miraculous that must be adjudicated by an appeal to the natural sciences. In any case I cannot see that this is an issue that must be resolved here and I am content to let the ambiguity ride. It seems to me that an intuitive distinction between the ordinary and the extraordinary will serve us perfectly well here.

In addition to requiring that a miracle be extraordinary, it must also express divine agency, and possess religious significance of a sort that will allow it to play some role in theistic religious practice. It may be an event that we cannot subsume under a deterministic natural law, but this is not necessary. Many lawful events might qualify as well. Indeed one of the most important points I wish to develop in this work is that *we do not have to find out* whether an event is consistent with natural law in order to refer rightly to it as a miracle.

In any case, as I have said, I am not concerned to defend a definition of 'miracle' with any rigor. I am more concerned to give a general idea of what might qualify. My principal concern is negative: I want to argue against a *supernaturalist* conception of the miraculous, and by way of providing an alternative account, I want to defend the conception of a miracle as a basic divine action, and to show how it is that our thinking of an event as a miracle involves incorporating it into a theistic religious practice.

Chapter 1

Miracles and the Laws of Nature

As I have tried to make clear in the Introduction, my purpose here is to argue for an account of miracles which (a) does not require that a miracle be a violation of natural law, or that it lack a natural cause, and (b) does not draw on the conception of a *supernatural* cause. I wish to construct a non-causal account of miracles. Before I do this, however, I want to show why such an account is necessary. This means showing what the liabilities are of the supernaturalist view.

Supernaturalist accounts of the miraculous sometimes attempt to make use of the conception of a miracle as violating the laws of nature. I begin, therefore, by examining the notion of a violation, and by considering, in particular, a line of argument defended by Alastair McKinnon and Antony Flew, for the claim that the notion of a violation of natural law is self-contradictory. At the heart of McKinnon's argument is the conception of the laws of nature as merely attempting to describe what actually happens in the world; the occurrence of an exception to some formulation of the laws of nature would show that formulation to be false. If McKinnon and Flew are correct about this, the supernaturalist cannot simultaneously assert the existence of the law, together with its exception, which is what is required if the event is to constitute a violation.

In response, Ninian Smart tries to rehabilitate the conception of a violation by construing it as a *nonrepeatable counterinstance* to the laws of nature. If the notion of a nonrepeatable counterinstance is simply that of an anomaly – that is, an event that is not determined to occur by antecedent physical circumstances – I have no objection.[1] Surely there is no incoherence involved in the suggestion that such events may occur. However, I do not see why we should refer to these events as violating anything. Their occurrence would only serve to show that nature is not fully deterministic.

Michael Levine argues that the laws of nature do not describe what happens in nature, but only what happens in the absence of any supernatural force. On Levine's view, supernaturally caused events may be understood as an intervention into the natural order, but are not, strictly speaking, *violations* of the laws of nature. I will animate, against Levine, an argument originating with Antony Flew, that there are no empirical criteria by which we might distinguish those anomalies that represent supernatural intrusions into the natural order from 'mere' anomalies, or spontaneous breakdowns in the natural order. If this argument is correct, then it shows, at minimum, that the supernaturalist faces an insurmountable epistemic problem in trying to show the inadequacy of naturalism; she lacks any ground for saying that an anomalous event is the effect of a supernatural intervention into the natural order.

The supernaturalist faces an additional problem as well. If there is no empirical distinction to be made between a supernatural intervention and a spontaneous breakdown of the natural order, it is difficult to make out the *conceptual* contrast between these (purportedly) different kinds of events. My argument here leaves open the possibility, however, that we may find the needed contrast by understanding supernatural interventions in teleological terms.

I should make it clear that I do not think the supernaturalist will be satisfied with either of my objections here. We might have reason to acknowledge the presence of a supernatural force if doing so will allow us to *explain* the occurrence of an event that fails to conform to natural law. My response to this line of argument must wait for a fuller discussion of the notion of a supernatural explanation, which will come in Chapter 3.

The Logical Impossibility of a Violation

The best known criticism of belief in miracles is due to David Hume. Hume's focus was on the credibility of testimony for the miraculous; he argued that, given the status of a miracle as a violation of natural law, no testimony could be strong enough to establish the occurrence of such an event. By contrast, more recent criticisms have been concerned with the very concept of a miracle. In particular, some have argued that the notion of a violation of natural law is self-contradictory. No one, of course, thinks that the report of an event that might be *taken* as a miracle, such as a resurrection, or a walking on water, is logically self-contradictory. Nevertheless some philosophers have argued that it is paradoxical to suggest both that such an event has occurred, *and* that it is a violation of natural law. This argument dates back at least as far as T. H. Huxley, who tells us that the definition of a miracle as contravening the order of nature 'is self-contradictory, because all we know of the order of nature is derived from our observation of the course of events of which the so-called miracle is a part' (1894: 157; Huxley is also quoted approvingly by Flew 1997: 202). Should an apparent miracle take place, such as a suspension in the air of a piece of lead, scientific methodology forbids us from supposing that any law of nature has been violated; on the contrary, Huxley tells us that 'the scientist would simply set to work to investigate the conditions under which so highly unexpected an occurrence took place; and modify his, hitherto, unduly narrow conception of the laws of nature' (1894: 156).

More recently this view has been defended by Antony Flew (1966, 1967, 1997) as well as by Alastair McKinnon. McKinnon has argued (1967) that the attempt to speak of violations of the law of nature results from an illegitimate attempt to transfer the concept of a violation from the domain of civil law to that of the laws of nature. The notion of a violation generally involves the suggestion that some agent has acted contrary to what the law specifies, but that the law continues to remain in force despite the contravention. It is easy to see how this can happen in regard to a statute; if I act contrary to the laws of my state in exceeding the speed limit, I do not thereby render invalid, or veto, the provision in the vehicle code that forbids me to do this. Thus the law continues in force despite the fact that I have acted contrary to it. But this is only possible because civil codes are prescriptive in their force; the law says that I ought not exceed the speed limit, but this is compatible with saying that I have in fact exceeded it.

The laws of nature, however, are not prescriptive in their force; they are merely attempts to describe what actually happens in nature. It is much harder, therefore, to show how such a law can survive the occurrence of an event that is contrary to it. Suppose a natural law (L) having the form 'All As are Bs'; for example, all objects made of lead (A) are objects that will fall when we let go of them (B). A violation would be represented by the occurrence of an A that is not a B, or in this case, an object made of lead that does not fall when we let go of it. Thus to assert that a violation of natural law has occurred is to say at once that all As are Bs, but to say at the same time that there exists some A that is not a B is to say, paradoxically, that all objects made of lead will fall when left unsupported, but that this object made of lead did not fall when left unsupported. Clearly we cannot have it both ways; should we encounter a piece of lead that does not fall, we will be forced to admit that it is not true that all objects made of lead will fall. As soon as we have the apparent exception, we lose the law. A counterinstance to some statement of natural law negates that statement; it shows that our understanding of natural law is incorrect and must be modified – which implies that no violation has occurred after all.

If McKinnon is right about this, then it is logically impossible that any violation of natural law should ever occur. Of course this does not mean that no one has ever parted the Red Sea, walked on water, or been raised from the dead; hence this criticism does not undermine the Christian belief that these events really did occur (Mavrodes 1985: 337). It implies only that these events, if they did occur, are not violations of natural law, and if we insist that a miracle must be a violation of natural law, then they would not be miracles.

I want to consider the defense of the notion of a violation that is offered by Ninian Smart, but we might pause first to consider why it should be important to the supernaturalist to defend the conception. Clearly, where one wishes to say that a miracle is a violation, the idea is to suggest that nature is an orderly place, with all events taking place in accordance with laws, as though nature were a kind of machine. A violation is conceived as being the sort of event that takes place when there is outside interference into the workings of the machine; as McKinnon points out, God's role is to 'give the machine such a bash that it skips a cog' (1967: 308). Thus the occurrence of an exception to natural law is supposed to signal the intrusion of an outside force or agency – one that is supernatural. The supernaturalist hopes to make the case that such an event would not be possible – or at least would be *unlikely* to occur – if nature is all there is. The occurrence of such an event will, she hopes, show that the naturalist cannot account for everything that happens in nature. The naturalistic account must be supplemented by reference to the supernatural.

It is crucial to the supernaturalist's case that we suppose nature to behave in a perfectly uniform fashion unless some supernatural force asserts itself. We must have reason to say, given the occurrence of an exception to nature's otherwise uniform working, that things would have gone on as they usually do were it not for a supernatural interference with the workings of nature.

Antony Flew argues (1984: 142) that the apologist must defend the conception of a miracle as a violation. For the apologist to point to a miracle as providing evidence for the existence of a transcendent God or the truth of a particular religious doctrine, we must not only have good reason to believe that it occurred, but also that it represents an overriding of natural law that originates from outside of nature. If this is correct, then we must (*per impossibile*) have both the law and the exception. As Flew puts the point, the apologist 'needs both the rule and the exception . . . It is no use for him to show that the universe is like *Hellzapoppin'*, where "anything may happen and it probably will"' (1997: 202). The supernaturalist will not be satisfied with the possibility that the universe is the sort of place in which *spontaneous* lapses occur in the natural order. This would rob her of the grounds for saying that the event in question would not have occurred in the absence of a supernatural intrusion. She must find some way to deny this possibility and argue that any such lapse must be due, or is probably due, to a supernatural intrusion.

Violations as Nonrepeatable Counterinstances to Natural Law

We have considered, as an objection to the concept of a violation of natural law, that it is logically self-contradictory. Let us now consider a response to this objection. Suppose we take it to be a law of nature that a human being cannot walk on water; subsequently, however, we become convinced that on one particular occasion (*O*), say for example, 18 April 1910, someone was actually able to do this. Yet suppose that after the occurrence of *O* water goes back to behaving exactly as we are accustomed to it behaving. In such a case our formulation of natural law would continue to have its usual predictive value, and it would continue to explain why, in all other cases, heavy objects have sunk. Under such circumstances, we would neither abandon our formulation of the law, nor would we revise it. The only revision possible in this case would be to say 'Human beings cannot walk on water, except on occasion *O*'. Yet the amendment in this case is entirely *ad hoc*; in its reference to a particular event, the revision fails to take the generalized form that statements of natural law normally possess, and it adds no explanatory power to the original formulation of the law. It gives us no better explanation of what has happened in the past, it does nothing to account for the exceptional event *O*, and it fares no better than the original formulation when it comes to predicting what will happen in the future. In this case *O* is a nonrepeatable counterinstance to natural law. Faced with such an event we would retain our old formulation of the law, which is to say that the exceptional event *O* does not negate it. This means that there is no contradiction implied by affirming the law together with its exception.

Things would be different if we can identify some feature (*F*) of the circumstances in which *O* occurred which will explain why *O* occurred in this one case when normally it would not. *F* might be some force operating to counteract the usual tendency of a dense object, such as a human body, to sink in water. In this case, on discovery of *F* we are in a position to reformulate the law in a fruitful way, saying that human beings cannot walk on water except when *F* is present. Since the exception in this case now has a generalized form (i.e. it expressed the proposition that if any human being walks on water, then F is present), our reformulation has the kind of generality that a statement of natural law ought to have. It explains the past interaction of dense bodies with water as well as the original formulation did, and it explains why someone was able to walk on water on occasion O. Finally, it will serve to predict what will happen in the future, both when F is absent and when it is present.

We may now, following Ninian Smart (1964: 37) and Richard Swinburne (1970: 26), understand a violation as a *nonrepeatable counterinstance* to natural law. We encounter a nonrepeatable counterinstance when someone walks on water, as in case O, and, reproducing the circumstances in which O occurred, no one is able to walk on water. Since a statement of natural law is falsified only by the occurrence of a repeatable counterinstance, it is paradoxical to assert a particular statement of law and at the same time proclaim that a *repeatable* counterinstance to it has occurred. However, if Smart and Swinburne are correct, there is no paradox in asserting the existence of the law together with the occurrence of a counterinstance that is not repeatable.

I want to make three objections to the notion of a miracle as a nonrepeatable counterinstance to the laws of nature. First, it seems to me that, repeatable or not, the occurrence of an A that is not a B *would*, contrary to what Smart says, falsify a law of the form 'All As are Bs'. Second, I want to argue that if the supernaturalist hopes to employ the conception of a violation as a nonrepeatable counterinstance, it will not help her to make the case for supernaturalism, since we have no empirical means of identifying an event as a nonrepeatable counterinstance to a law of nature. Finally, I want to show that, even if we could identify an event as a nonrepeatable counterinstance to the laws of nature, we would have no reason to speak of it as anything more than a mere anomaly, or an event that is not determined by any physical antecedent; the conception of a nonrepeatable counterinstance is an empty one.

Objection 1: Nonrepeatable Counterinstances as Falsifying a Law

Suppose once again some law of nature (L) having the form 'All As are Bs'. Smart wants to say that, if we encountered a single counterinstance to such a law – some A that was not a B – we would continue to employ this law as long as the counterinstance was not a repeatable one. The occurrence of a nonrepeatable counterinstance does not force us to reformulate the law. However, it is far from clear that this means we would continue to suppose that L is true. It may be that we would continue to predict that future As will be Bs. But this does not commit us to saying that L is true. There are two alternatives.

First, we can continue to suppose that future As will be Bs based on the overwhelming *likelihood* that this will be the case. But then, all we need for this is to say, not that all As are Bs, but that the vast majority of As are Bs. The fact that we continue to predict that As will be Bs does not require us to admit that L is true; it is compatible with the weaker generalization (L^*) that *most* As are Bs, or that some percentage of As are Bs. And of course the occurrence of an A that is not a B will not constitute an exception to the reformulated law L^*, which now assumes the form of a statistical generalization. On the contrary, it is subsumable under L^*. Thus we have no violation; that is, we do not have that for which Smart is searching, namely, the law together with its exception. The supernaturalist, when she says that something is a violation of natural law, has to find some way to defend the suggestion that this A would have been a B had it not been for the intrusion of a supernatural influence. But if the operations of nature are to be described statistically, she loses her ground for saying this.[2]

A second option is to concede that the occurrence of an A that is not a B does falsify L, but that we continue to employ L because, despite being false, it is *useful*. It may be that this is simply how it is with nature; it operates in fits and starts, running smoothly for a time and then, inexplicably, hiccupping. In this case we have no alternative but to employ those generalizations that come as close to this as possible. Once again we are deprived of being able to have a (true) law of nature together with its exception. And if this is simply how it is with nature, there is no need to resort to any talk of supernatural intrusions.

Objection 2: Identifying Nonrepeatable Counterinstances

In considering the possibility that a nonrepeatable counterinstance to natural law has occurred, we will have great difficulty *determining* whether an event is nonrepeatable. Let us return to our example, *O*, walking on water, which will be nonrepeatable just in case no one is able to walk on water when the circumstances of *O* have been reproduced. But the problem will be in determining whether those circumstances have, in fact, been reproduced. For in order to reproduce them, we must be certain that we have identified all of the causally relevant factors in the circumstances surrounding *O*. However, given the fact that there might be some unknown causal factor at work in those circumstances, making it possible for *O* to occur on just that occasion, we cannot be certain that we have done this.

This observation leads us into a problem for the miracle apologist that was posed by Antony Flew. Flew (1966, 1967, 1997) speaks of this as the Problem of Identifying Miracles. He has argued that, in order to have any apologetic force, a supernaturalistic appeal to miracles must find some empirical ground for identifying an event as a violation of natural law – for saying, that is, that an event is one that could not occur had nature been left to its own devices.

Now let us suppose that we are confronted with an event that, following Smart and Swinburne, we would like to say is a nonrepeatable counterinstance to natural law. The problem is to show that it is not a *repeatable* counterinstance. Consider once again the example of someone walking on water. This will be a repeatable counterinstance just in case there is some natural force operating to make it possible that someone walks on water when otherwise they would not be able to do so. But the problem that faces us is that there may be some such force present which is as yet unknown to us. The epistemic dilemma in which we find ourselves is to distinguish between a case in which there is *no* natural force operating to produce the apparent exception, and one in which there is an *unknown* force operating.

It seems clear that this is not a distinction that can be made on empirical grounds. Surely there is no observation we might make in order to eliminate the possibility that some unknown natural force is operating in a particular case. Observations may reveal the presence of a natural cause – this is something that the scientist can discover; thus the possibility will always remain that we might discover a natural force that makes it possible for someone to walk on water, however remote this possibility might seem. We might also be able to eliminate the possibility that some *particular* cause is absent; for example, if we think some phenomenon might be due to the effects of radiation, we can eliminate this possibility by providing the appropriate shielding. But we have no way to control for the possibility that some *unknown* natural cause is at work.

Indeed, matters become even worse if we are entitled to assume that events in nature generally conform to laws of nature, which is the assumption that the supernaturalist wishes to make in the context of arguing for the occurrence of violations. In this case, the very occurrence of an apparent counterinstance will be evidence that some unknown physical force is operating. And surely this is how the natural scientist would view the matter.

Richard Swinburne, defending Smart's conception of a miracle as a nonrepeatable counterinstance, attempts a solution to this difficulty. He admits that any judgement that an event is nonrepeatable will be corrigible, but insists that

> 'You could be wrong' is a knife that cuts both ways. What seem to be perfectly explicable events might prove, when we come to know the laws of nature much better, to be violations. But of course this is not very likely. The reasonable man goes by the available evidence here, and also in the converse case. He supposes that what is, on all evidence, a violation of natural laws really is one. (1979: 230ff.)

If I understand Swinburne correctly here, he wants to argue that, if I let go of a bowling ball and it falls to the floor, it is possible that there was some unknown natural force operating that would have had the effect that the ball would remain suspended in the air; in this case, the ball's falling, in accordance with our expectations, would be a violation of natural law. But of course we have no obligation to eliminate the possibility that some unknown force was operating in this case. Swinburne seems to want to argue, then, that it is equally wrong to suppose that we have a similar obligation in the case of an apparent violation. We take an event that is *prima facie* in conformity with the laws of nature to be in conformity with those laws; so, it seems, we ought to take an event that *prima facie* fails to conform to the laws of nature to be a violation, i.e. a nonrepeatable counterinstance.

What Swinburne fails to appreciate here is the force of our usual assumption that events in nature generally conform to laws of nature. It is not as though we typically work without any presuppositions regarding the laws of nature, so that we might be as well inclined to judge that a given event is a violation as we would be to suppose that it is lawlike. On the contrary, our presumption is in favor of natural law, as surely even Swinburne will concede.[3] Nor does this presumption beg the question against one who, like Swinburne, wishes to assert the possibility of occasional violations. Indeed it is hard to see why an event ought to be considered a violation if nature were not *ordinarily* lawful, and if it is ordinarily lawful we will suppose that, all things being equal, any given event conforms to natural law.

I have argued that we lack any empirical grounds for making a distinction between a counterinstance to some law of nature that is repeatable, and one that is not. As Flew has argued, we cannot point to the occurrence of a violation of the laws of nature as evidence for a supernatural order if we cannot, in the first place, identify any event as a violation; defining 'violation' as a nonrepeatable counterinstance does not seem to help.

I can imagine a critic objecting here that an event which appears to be contrary to the laws of nature may occur in circumstances which make it likely to be an expression of divine agency. Suppose, for example, that immediately after giving a sermon, Saint Polly begins to levitate off the ground, and a loud voice, apparently emanating from the heavens, is heard to proclaim: 'I am The Lord. I have levitated Polly as a sign that she speaks with divine authority. Follow her.' It is all well and good to say that there might be some unknown natural force operating to make this possible, and so that this event might be, for all we know, capable of being explained by reference to natural forces. But there appears to be a supernatural explanation at hand which obviates the need to seek a natural one.

This is an important response, and one that deserves some careful unpacking. I will postpone an extended discussion of the notion of a supernatural explanation until Chapter 3. Nevertheless some immediate observations are possible. First, we should notice that this response, in its appeal to divine agency, represents the introduction of teleological considerations in the identification of an event as miraculous. Since I wish to argue for a teleological approach, I take this to be a significant development; I will be satisfied if I have, at this point, begun to show the need for taking a teleological approach to the miraculous. Second, this response assumes that any reason we have for supposing that God is responsible for Polly's levitation will be reason to suppose that this levitation is a nonrepeatable counterinstance to natural law – i.e. a violation. But it is not obvious that divine agency precludes the possibility that there is some unknown natural force operating in Polly's levitation. I will have more to say about this in Chapter 4, where I will argue that we may identify an event as expressing divine agency *without* saying anything about its relation to the laws of nature.

Objection 3: Counterinstance as Anomaly

We have considered Alastair McKinnon's argument that it is logically self-contradictory to assert that a violation of natural law has occurred, and we have examined Ninian Smart's response, which is to stipulate that a violation is a nonrepeatable counterinstance to the laws of nature. In the last section I argued that we could never have any empirical grounds for distinguishing a nonrepeatable counterinstance from one that was repeatable, but was due to the operation of some unknown physical force. We seem to have no means of eliminating the possibility that such an unknown force is operating.

I want now to grant, for the sake of argument, that we *could* eliminate this possibility. Suppose we were able to determine, once and for all, that there was no natural force operating to produce the exception. In this case the event would constitute an *anomaly*. By this I mean to say that it would not be an instance of any deterministic law of nature.[4] But an anomaly is not the same thing as a *violation* of natural law, and the occurrence of such an event would not be evidence for the existence of any supernatural order. The occurrence of such an event would only force us to admit that the universe does not fully conform to deterministic laws of the form 'All As are Bs'.[5] But this hypothesis is fully compatible with naturalism in either of the forms we have made mention of here. It does not force us to deny ontological naturalism, and admit the existence of non-natural forces or entities; nor does it require us to deny methodological naturalism, and suppose that the methods of the natural sciences must be supplemented by any form of supernaturalistic mode of inquiry. Indeed as far as I understand these things, modern physics *already* acknowledges that some events, such as those involving subatomic particles, are not fully determined by physical forces.[6] Our discovery of such events has not brought us to acknowledge that the laws of nature are, after all, frequently violated; on the contrary, it has caused us to change our understanding of the laws of nature to accommodate these events. And as far as I know, this change in our understanding does not enable us to predict, with any greater accuracy, the states of subatomic particles. It simply accommodates the fact that we cannot predict these states with any great degree of precision. Naturalism, in other words, is entirely comfortable with the proposition that events in nature are not fully determined.

It is possible that the supernaturalist may reply here simply by saying that all she means, by her reference to violations of the laws of nature, is to pick out that class of events that are not determined to occur by physical forces, and which for that reason cannot be subsumed under the laws of nature. In other words she may stipulate that 'violation' is synonymous with 'anomaly', as I am using that term here to describe an event that is not determined to occur by antecedent physical circumstances. But that is a rather large concession, and is clearly not one that either Smart or Swinburne have been willing to make. Because the occurrence of such an event is compatible with a naturalistic worldview, this undermines the supernaturalist's ability to argue that the event in question would not have occurred had it not been for the intrusion of a supernatural influence of some kind. This was the notion of a violation that I set out, at the beginning of this chapter, to discredit.

A Supernaturalistic Conception of Natural Law

I am attempting to provide objections against a supernaturalistic approach to miracles, by which a miracle is understood as an event that requires us to reject the tenets of naturalism. The occurrence of such an event would give us reason to think that one or more entities exist that cannot be described as *natural* entities; that causes operate on natural objects that cannot be described as *natural* causes; that explanations may be given for events in nature that are not consistent with the methods of the natural sciences. One way to defend such a supernaturalistic approach is to argue that a miracle is a violation of natural law. If all that is meant by this is that a miracle is an anomaly – an event that fails to instantiate any law of nature – I have no objection. However, the usual conception of a violation is the conception of an event that 'cuts across the ways of nature . . . or the real grain of the world' (McKinnon 1967: 308). Since the occurrence of an anomaly shows that the world is not fully governed by natural law, its occurrence cannot constitute this kind of disturbance in the natural order.

Much of the trouble that we have seen befall supernaturalism comes from the suggestion that the laws of nature merely describe what happens in the world. It is open to the supernaturalist, however, to take another approach; she may insist that rather than describing what actually happens in nature, the laws of nature only tell us what happens in the absence of any supernatural cause. On this view, the scope of natural law is limited to those events that have natural causes. Natural laws do not have the form 'All As are Bs', but instead say that 'All As are Bs unless some supernatural force is in operation'. The occurrence of an A that is not a B would not represent a violation of a law of nature so long as it is the result of a supernatural force. Thus the supernaturalist may abandon the conception of a miracle as a violation of natural law, and still hope to maintain what is most crucial to her view – the notion of a miracle as something that would not have occurred without the intrusion of a supernatural influence.

Michael Levine defends this view of the laws of nature:

> Suppose the laws of nature are regarded as nonuniversal or incomplete in the sense that while they cover natural events, they do not cover, and are not intended to cover, non-natural events such as supernaturally caused events if there are or could be any. A physically impossible occurrence would not violate a law of nature because it would not be covered by (i.e. within the scope of) such a law. (1989: 67)

On Levine's understanding, a physically impossible event would be one that could not occur given the influence of only physical, or natural, causes. But what is physically impossible is not absolutely impossible, since such an event might occur as the result of a *supernatural* cause. One way to understand this is to say that all laws must ultimately be understood as disjunctions, of the form 'All As are Bs unless some supernatural cause is operating'. (Let us refer to this as the *supernaturalistic* formulation of law, as opposed to a *naturalistic* formulation which simply asserts that all As are Bs without taking account of the possibility of any supernatural cause.) If this is correct, then it turns out that strictly speaking, though a miracle may be contrary to natural regularities, i.e. to those regularities that may be observed when only natural forces are operating, it is not a violation of natural law after all, since it is something that occurs by means of a supernatural intervention. Furthermore, since statements of natural law are only intended to describe what happens in the absence of supernatural intrusions, the occurrence of a miracle does not negate any formulation of natural law.

The supernaturalistic conception of natural law suggests that the evidence for natural laws, gathered when supernatural causes are absent, does not weigh against the possibility of miracles, since miracles are the result of supernatural interventions into the natural order. Thus there is a failure of analogy between those cases that form the basis for our statements of natural law, and the circumstances of a miracle. Our expectations about what may happen in nature, when these are based on our experience of what happens in the absence of any supernatural cause, do not apply in circumstances in which such a cause is operating.

Identifying Supernatural Intrusions: An Objection

We have been examining the supernaturalistic conception of a miracle as an event that cannot occur if nature is to be left to its own devices; its occurrence signals the existence of a supernatural force or entity and is something that cannot be explained in accordance with the methods of the natural sciences. In particular, we are considering Michael Levine's contention that a miracle lies outside the scope of natural law, since natural laws only describe what happens in nature when no supernatural force is operating.

I want to present an objection to Levine's account, which is that I do not see how it can escape Flew's Problem of Identifying Miracles. Let us recall Flew's argument: He wants to say that if a miracle is to serve any apologetic purpose, as evidence for the truth of some revelation, then it must be possible to identify it as an event that could not have taken place had nature been operating on its own, i.e. without a supernatural intervention on the part of God; furthermore these criteria must be natural, or observable.

Suppose an extraordinary event occurs, which the supernaturalist would like to attribute to a cause that comes from beyond the natural world; here is something that, in the absence of a supernatural intrusion, would not have occurred. The following two states of affairs are empirically indistinguishable:

1. The event is the result of an unknown natural cause.
2. The event is the result of a supernatural cause.

This, of course, is due to the fact that we do not observe the cause of the event in either of these cases – in the first, it is because the cause is unknown to us, and in the second, because supernatural causes are unobservable *ex hypothesi*. Thus the issue here is whether we should suppose that our failure to observe any cause for the event is due to our inability to fully identify all of the natural forces that were operating to produce it, or whether it is because the cause, being supernatural, is unobservable in principle. The problem in this case seems to be an epistemic one. At least, our difficulty in determining whether or not (1) is the case is an epistemic one; we simply do not know whether there may be a natural cause operating and we do not seem to have the means to eliminate this possibility. We might, of course, determine, after sufficient investigation, that there *is* a previously unknown natural cause in operation. But we can never find out that there is none. It will always be an open possibility that some such cause is present and will be revealed to some future investigation.

The problem becomes even more acute if we recognize that there is a third possibility in addition to the other two:

3. The event *has* no cause; its occurrence is random or spontaneous, i.e. it is what we have referred to as an anomaly.

Now we find ourselves in the following predicament. Suppose that some wildly extraordinary event occurs, e.g. the cities of San Francisco and Boston suddenly switch places, so that San Francisco is now on the Atlantic Ocean, and Boston on the Pacific. It may be intuitively tempting to say that we could be quite confident that this is not something that could result from any natural force, though it may be hard to argue for this claim. It is true that any natural force capable of bringing about such an event would be radically unlike any that we have previously encountered. But it is not clear why it would be better here to say that some *supernatural* force, of a sort that is completely different from any we have hitherto encountered, is responsible; indeed if we are going to hypothesize the existence of previously unknown forces, it would be more parsimonious to stick with a *natural* one. In any case, let us set this point aside and, for the sake of argument, suppose that we have good reason to eliminate the possibility that any natural force is involved with the sudden relocation of these two cities. What is to stop us from simply concluding that the event *has* no cause?

The point here is that it does not follow from the fact that some event lacks a natural cause that it must have one that is supernatural, unless we can assume that all events have some cause or another. The naturalist is free to deny this. Naturalism does not commit the skeptic to suppose that every event in nature has a cause; it only commits him to the view that, *insofar as we can speak of events as having causes,* we can speak of them as having natural causes. The naturalism of the skeptic only commits him to saying that, insofar as events in nature may be explained, they may be given *natural* explanations. And the possibility of his adopting this position makes things very difficult for the supernaturalist. For even if the skeptic may somehow be forced to admit the occurrence of some event that lacks any natural cause, all that seems to be required is that he concede that this is just the way it is with nature: It is not fully law-governed. This places a burden on the supernaturalist to give reasons for supposing that lapses in the natural order have a supernatural cause, as opposed to their having no cause at all. The problem for the supernaturalist is to show that this event is one that cannot happen without the intrusion of a supernatural force. But if the universe is not fully law-governed, *anything* can happen, even if there are no entities or forces save natural ones.

Now let me emphasize here that I am not suggesting we might somehow *discover* that an event has no cause. It is important to see that such a conclusion could never be the result of an empirical investigation. It is not as though we possess a finite list of things to check, in trying to find the cause of an event, so that when we get to the bottom of the list we know that we have examined every possibility and can now proclaim with confidence that the event is causeless. We will always be in a position of having to allow that the event might have a cause that eludes us. For similar reasons, an empirical investigation will never tell us that an event has no *natural* cause. We will always have to admit the possibility in principle that the event has a natural cause that is resistant to discovery. Certainly the scientific method contains no provision for identifying an event as being beyond its power to explain, or for saying that it must forever represent a gap, a missing piece in the puzzle-picture of the world. Hence Flew's observation that there are no empirical criteria by which we can determine that an event is one that can only occur with the help of a transcendent power.

Of course someone might, after an extensive investigation, finally say: 'I give up. This event simply has no cause!' But this would surely be nothing more than an expression of frustration, and of a resignation to desist from the search.

Supernatural Intrusions: Lost Contrast

I have said that we have no empirical means of distinguishing between cases (2) and (3) above – no empirical means, that is, of distinguishing a case in which an anomalous event has a supernatural cause, and thus represents an intrusion into the domain of nature – and one in which it has no cause at all. At minimum this implies an epistemic problem for a defender of supernaturalism; given the occurrence of an anomaly, there seems to be no way of knowing whether it has a supernatural cause, or whether it has no cause at all, representing nothing more than a spontaneous breakdown of the natural order. If so, this means that the notion of a supernatural cause is useless to the apologist, who would employ it in the attempt to persuade us that nature is not all there is.

I think, however, that there is a deeper problem here. If there is, in principle, no empirical criterion by which we can distinguish a supernaturally caused anomaly from one that has no cause at all, it is reasonable to ask *what it means* to speak of an anomaly as having a supernatural cause. If, in describing some event as supernaturally caused, we intend to say that it is more than a mere anomaly, then we ought to be able to make clear just what, in addition, we are saying when we describe it in this way. The question I want to ask here is: What is *added* to the conception of an anomaly by describing it as having a supernatural cause? And, given that a mere anomaly, i.e. a spontaneous lapse in the natural order, is indistinguishable from one that has a supernatural cause, I think the answer is that *nothing* is added.

Now I must hasten to forestall an objection here. The description of an event as supernaturally caused is quite often taken as synonymous with a description of that event as expressing supernatural agency; typically this would be understood as *divine* agency. I do not wish to deny that when we associate an event with divine agency, we are saying something interesting about it; quite to the contrary. I acknowledge the contrast between the world of Hellzapoppin' (as Flew puts it), in which nature suffers spontaneous lapses in its order, and a world in which anomalies may be attributed to divine agency. I *do* wish to deny that the description of an event as supernaturally caused is synonymous with the description of it as a divine action; I will argue in detail for this position in Chapter 4. In the meantime I will be content to make a narrow point, which is that, *aside* from the prospect of associating an anomaly with divine agency, nothing is added by describing it as having a supernatural cause. It is only by speaking of an anomaly as an expression of divine agency that we can provide a meaningful contrast to an event that is nothing more than a spontaneous breakdown in the natural order.

Perhaps an analogy will help to illustrate the problem here. Suppose I were to introduce the notion of a *sapple*. A sapple is a variety of apple; what sets it apart from ordinary apples is that it possesses property S. However, having property S makes no difference whatsoever to the appearance of any apple that possesses it. As far as their observable properties go, sapples are completely indistinguishable from ordinary apples. This means, of course, that we have no means of determining whether any given apple is just an ordinary apple, or a sapple. Now we might say that the problem here is an epistemic one; perhaps the difficulty is simply that we have no way of *knowing* which of the apples are sapples. But it seems to me that there is also a conceptual issue here. What we ought to say is that, at least up to this point, we have been unable to articulate any real contrast between sapples and ordinary apples. It would be wrong to respond by protesting that after all, sapples possess property S; the distinction is empty. That is, unless an apple's possession of S is capable, at least in principle, of making some difference in our experience, it adds nothing to our description of an apple to say that it has this property.

We might imagine an objection here, however, which is that we really haven't tried to give any particular content to the supposed distinction between sapples and ordinary apples. Perhaps it depends upon what S is taken to represent. So let us try to fill this out a bit; let us suppose that S is the property of possessing a particular sort of worm. However, it is not just any kind of worm I have in mind here. Let us say that an apple possesses S just in case it is inhabited by a *supernatural* worm. It is important, of course, that such a worm be empirically undetectable. It is invisible, and has neither extension nor mass. It does not leave a hole in the apples that it inhabits; indeed it does not affect them in any manner that may be revealed to our observation. It is always a possibility, we might say, that – when we bite into an apple – this may be no ordinary apple but a sapple, an apple inhabited by a supernatural worm. However, where we might be squeamish about the possibility that our apple is inhabited by an ordinary worm, it seems to me that its being inhabited by a supernatural worm makes no difference at all. If someone were to suggest to me that every apple I had ever eaten was in fact a sapple, I would not mind in the least. When it comes to worms, it is the prospect of the empirical discovery that is disquieting.

Now I think we ought to say that, by cashing S out in terms of supernatural worms, we should not in fact suppose that we have provided any content to the notion of a sapple, despite the fact that we may have a very clear idea of what an *ordinary* worm is like. The problem here is that in attempting to qualify the notion of wormhood supernaturally, we have deprived our supposed worm of the chance to have any of the properties that are normally associated with worms, such as having a particular color, size, shape, mass and so on. And I think we can say precisely the same thing of a supernatural *cause*. A supernatural cause cannot be contiguous in space or time with its effect. Its operation cannot be mediated through any physical force such as gravitation or magnetism. Just as there is nothing left of our worm, once we remove all of its physical properties, so there is nothing left of the notion of a cause when we attempt to locate it outside the domain of nature. We will take a closer look at these issues in the next chapter.

A Supernaturalistic Response

I do not suppose that I have given a knockdown argument against the possibility that what appear to us, in the natural world, as anomalies may be the result of supernatural causes. I will continue to make my case in Chapters 2 and 3. Before proceeding, however – in order to map out the territory – I want to consider briefly how a supernaturalist might respond to what I have said here.

One possibility is that she will argue that an anomaly may occur in circumstances that make it reasonable to attribute it to divine agency. The supernaturalist may insist that an appeal to divine agency gives us the hope of *explaining* the event, where no explanation would otherwise be available. Thus the reference to a supernatural cause is justified by its explanatory power. The contrast between a supernaturally caused event and a mere anomaly lies in the fact that a supernaturally caused event has an explanation where a mere anomaly, or a spontaneous lapse in the natural order, is inexplicable.

The full response to this line of argument will occupy me over the course of the next two chapters. However, some brief preliminary remarks are in order. First, let us notice the shift to a teleological appeal; I want to argue that we ought to conceive miracles teleologically, as expressions of divine agency, and also that doing this requires a consideration of the context in which they occur. I have no objection to this response as far as it embraces these points. If my criticism of supernaturalism has forced it into speaking of supernatural causation in teleological terms, I will be content.

Two questions remain, however. First: What sort of explanatory force comes with attributing an extraordinary event to a supernatural cause? I will consider this question more carefully in Chapter 3.

The second question I wish to raise may seem an odd one, given the routine assumption that anything that can be attributed to divine agency may automatically be considered as having a supernatural cause. Those who would defend a supernaturalistic picture of miracles generally seem to suppose (A) that God is a supernatural being, and (B) that if x may be attributed to God's agency, then God causes x to occur. Thus attributing x to divine agency amounts to saying that it has a supernatural cause. I will not challenge supposition (A), though I think it is reasonable to ask for clarification of what it means to *say* that God is a supernatural being. I do, however, wish to challenge (B). The primary fallacy of the supernaturalist is, I think, precisely the fact that she conflates the question of divine agency with the issue of supernatural causation. I will address this problem in detail in Chapter 4. I turn now to a closer examination of the notion of a supernatural cause.

Chapter 2

Miracles and Causes

My goal in this present work is to argue against a supernaturalistic conception of 'miracle'. I want to argue that a miracle need not be understood as being in any sense contrary to nature; in particular, I wish to deny that we must conceive it to be a violation of natural law, or that we must take it as having a supernatural cause. Of course part of my task is to show that there is a dividend to be enjoyed in rejecting such a conception, and to this end I am trying to show the problems that come with it. I hope first to show what the liabilities are with the supernaturalistic conception of 'miracle', and then offer an account that escapes these.

A brief recapitulation is in order of what we have done so far. First, I have tried to show the problems that come with an account of miracles as violations of natural law. The supernaturalist typically wants to point to the occurrence of a violation as implying the inadequacy of naturalism. I have conceded that there is no obscurity in the suggestion that an event may occur that cannot be subsumed under natural law. I have referred to such an event as an *anomaly*, by which I mean an event that is not determined to occur by physical circumstances. I do not know how we could ever discover that an event falls into this category; we have no way of distinguishing mere anomalies from events that are due to unknown natural forces. In any case it seems, contrary to the argument of Ninian Smart, that it is reasonable to take the occurrence of such an event as showing that events in nature are not fully lawlike. If this is true, then there is no reason to suppose that such an event would be properly considered as a violation of anything – that it 'cuts across' the natural order – or to suppose that it is incompatible with the claims of naturalism.

I then considered a *supernaturalistic* account of the laws of nature, as this is defended by Michael Levine. Such an account seeks to argue that the laws of nature only describe how things will be in the absence of any supernatural force. I attempted to show that Levine's account suffers from a problem, which is that we have no empirical means of identifying an event as being one that could not occur without the intrusion of some supernatural force. There are no observable criteria by which we can determine that an event is the effect of a supernatural cause, as opposed to it having an unknown *natural* cause. This represents a substantial epistemic problem for the supernaturalist. She wants to point to the occurrence of an anomaly as reason for believing that a supernatural force is at work. But she can offer us no means of distinguishing cases in which such a force is present from those that are due to unknown natural causes.

The supernaturalist faces a further difficulty arising from the fact that an event may simply have no cause at all, that is, that it may be an anomaly. I have argued that this possibility brings with it a conceptual problem. Given that there is, in principle, no empirical distinction to be made between an anomaly that is supernaturally caused, and one that is not, the notion of a supernatural cause seems to be empty. The question we may ask here is, what is added to the conception of an anomaly when we say that it has a supernatural cause? There may seem to be an obvious answer to this question: We think of it as having a *cause.* However, while the concept of an event's having a *natural* cause has a clear sense, it is far from obvious that it can retain this sense when we transplant it to the context of the supernatural. This question will be a central concern of the present chapter.

In this chapter I will focus on the suggestion that a miracle is an event with a supernatural cause. Before I proceed, however, I should make clear that there are two issues that I am postponing. In particular, there are two ways in which one might try to defend the idea that a miracle is a supernaturally caused event. One of these is to say that we are entitled to refer to an event as supernaturally caused when it is capable of receiving a supernatural explanation. This is a possibility I will consider in Chapter 3. Another is to say that we may identify something as supernaturally caused when it occurs in circumstances that suggest that it is an expression of divine agency – i.e. when it can be attributed to the will of God. I will examine this suggestion in more detail in Chapter 4.

Thus, what I propose to do now is to examine more carefully the notion of supernatural causation. As we noticed at the close of the last chapter, the supernaturalist faces a dilemma in making out the notion of a supernatural cause. If she construes this as too closely analogous to a natural cause, then she will be hard-pressed to say what is *supernatural* about it. On the other hand, if a supernatural cause bears no resemblance at all to the sort of causes we find in nature, we may wonder why we should refer to them as causes – or indeed, whether the notion of a supernatural cause has any content at all. A further difficulty is that if the supernatural entities that are supposed to have causal efficacy in the natural world are conceived as being too different from natural entities, it will be hard to say how there can be any causal interaction between nature and the supernatural. In this case, a metaphysical problem emerges that is similar to the one encountered by the substance dualist, when she attempts to account for the interaction between mind and body.

What is a Supernatural Cause?

I have said that I propose to examine the conception of a supernatural cause. In particular, I am concerned about what we add to the conception of an anomaly – an event that is not an instance of any law of nature – by saying that it is supernaturally caused. Now I should confess before I start that I find this difficult to do, and the problem is, I would argue, that the concept of a supernatural cause is confused. It is also not clear that everyone who uses the term means the same thing by it. In many instances when someone says that God is the supernatural cause of some event E, they only mean to say that E is something *done by* God or that it is an expression of God's will. Such an account of divine causation will be essentially an intentional, or *teleological* account. If this is all that is meant by a supernatural cause, then I have little objection to the notion, though I will argue in Chapter 4 that it is a mistake to suppose that every case of a divine *doing* is a case of divine *causing*. In other words, we may assert that something is *done by* God without saying that God is its *cause*, and I advocate that when all we intend to do is to attribute an event to divine agency, we can avoid confusion by refraining from speaking in terms of divine causation. The attempt to conflate these two issues – whether *x* is done by God, and whether God caused *x* – is, I think, at the heart of the difficulties that beset the supernaturalist account.

Often, however, the supernaturalist wants to make the operation of supposed supernatural causes closely analogous to the way in which natural causes operate, and of course we do not typically speak of natural causes in teleological terms. My primary concern in the present chapter will be to show the liabilities that attend the notion of such a supernatural cause.

As I see it, the defender of supernatural causation faces a dilemma, i.e. she has two options, either of which leads to an unfortunate result. Suppose, in trying to flesh out her conception of a supernatural cause, the supernaturalist paints a picture of the supernatural which turns out to be closely analogous to the realm of nature. She will then have trouble distinguishing supernatural causes from natural ones – that is, it will become difficult to say what is *supernatural* about the causes she invokes. In this case the distinction she wants to draw between natural and supernatural causes is empty; the supernatural collapses into the natural.

Faced with this prospect, the supernaturalist may try to paint a picture of supernatural entities, and supernatural causes, that maintains a sharp distinction between nature and the supernatural. If she takes this horn of the dilemma, she faces two additional problems. The first problem is conceptual. If supernatural causes are *too* different from natural ones – if there is no basis for their comparison to natural causes – it becomes difficult to say why supernatural causation deserves to be called 'causation' at all, or indeed, what is even *meant* by the notion of a supernatural cause. The second problem is a metaphysical one. Once again, if the realm of the supernatural becomes radically different from that of nature, the supernaturalist encounters a problem similar to that encountered by substance dualism; it becomes difficult to say how there can be any causal interaction between nature and the supernatural.

Nature as Causally Open

Let us pursue our understanding of supernatural causation by considering the idea that the natural universe is causally open to influences from the outside, i.e. from the supernatural. Although J. L. Mackie is a skeptic when it comes to belief in miracles, he – unlike Flew – agrees with the apologist that the conception of an intervention into natural law is a cogent one. The universe might have been constructed in such a way as to allow for supernatural interventions into nature; it is just that, as a contingent matter, it is not. He explains:

> There is no obscurity in the notion of intervention. Even in the natural world we have a clear understanding of how there can be for a time a closed system, in which everything that happens results from factors within that system in accordance with its laws of working, but how then something may intrude from outside it, bringing about changes that the system would not have produced of its own accord, so that things go on after this intrusion differently from how they would have gone on if the system had remained closed. All we need do, then, is to regard the whole natural world as being, for most of the time, such a closed system; we can then think of a supernatural intervention as something that intrudes into that system from outside the natural world as a whole. (1982: 21)

Quite often writers on the subject of miracles concern themselves with the issue of whether the natural universe is an open, or a closed, system. The supernaturalist typically wants to affirm that nature is an open system, and by this she means that it is *causally* open; she wants to claim that, at least on some occasions,[1] events in nature are subject to causal influences originating beyond or outside of it, which is to say, they are subject to the influence of *supernatural* causes. The term 'cause' may, of course, be used in a number of different ways. What concerns us here – and what is the primary focus of this chapter – is the question of just how closely our talk of an event as caused by God can be understood as analogous to the kind of causal language we find in the natural sciences.

Mackie, in his description of 'open universe' supernaturalism,[2] suggests that so long as the universe is not being acted upon from the outside, everything that occurs in nature may be attributed to natural causes and may be subsumed under natural law. If this is how things stand, then the occurrence of any event that fails to conform to natural law is one that may be inferred as having a supernatural cause. As we noticed in the last chapter, however, it is at least *logically* possible that events may occur that have no natural causes and which do not conform to any natural law, without their being the result of any force emanating from beyond nature. It is open to the naturalist to hold that the universe is causally closed, but that anomalies may occur nevertheless. The naturalist, by insisting that the universe is causally closed, is not committed to the claim that every event in nature may be subsumed under natural law. Accordingly, we ought to understand the open-universe position as advocating not only that events may occur that lack any natural cause, i.e. that there are gaps in the natural order, but that these gaps are, at least in some cases, the effects of supernatural causes.

Many contemporary theists speak of the universe as being open, though I would not claim that they all mean the same thing by this; it would surely be a mistake to suppose that just because someone proposes that the universe is an open one, they mean to say that it is susceptible to supernatural causes that are in any way closely analogous to the kinds of causes that are the subject of scientific inquiry. Keith Ward, for example, speaks of theology as embracing the 'death of the closed universe',[3] and claims that the occurrence of a miracle implies the intrusion of a 'new force' into nature (1990: 93). Robert Larmer (1996) argues that miracles are made possible by the fact that the universe is not a causally closed system. William Alston (1994: 50) argues that 'the laws we have reasons to accept lay down sufficient conditions only within a "closed system", that is, a system closed to influences other than those specified by the law'. He clearly wants to take seriously the possibility that nature may be susceptible to the operations of 'divine force' which makes events possible that otherwise would not be if nature were closed to outside influences. Thomas Tracy (2000: 310) argues that 'if we wish to affirm . . . that God acts in history, then there are good reasons to think that the world God has made will have an open ("gappy") structure'.[4]

C. S. Lewis gives a classic exposition of an open-universe conception of miracles by means of a very instructive analogy, and I propose to continue my discussion of the traditional causal view of miracles using this analogy. Nature, says Lewis, is like an aquarium. The environment in an aquarium functions for the most part autonomously, but from time to time things happen within the aquarium that have causes that lie outside of it.

> The behaviour of fishes which are being studied in a tank makes a relatively closed system. Now suppose that the tank is shaken by a bomb in the neighbourhood of the laboratory. The behaviour of the fishes will now be no longer fully explicable by what was going on in the tank before the bomb fell: there will be a failure of backward interlocking. This does not mean that the bomb and the previous history of events within the tank are totally and finally unrelated. It does mean that to find their relation you must go back to the much larger reality that includes both the tank and the bomb – the reality of wartime England in which bombs are falling but some laboratories are still at work. You would never find it within the history of the tank. In the same way, the miracle is not naturally interlocked in the backward direction. To find out how it is interlocked with the previous history of Nature you must replace both Nature and the miracle in a larger context.[5]

The analogy here is quite clear. Lewis intends for the fish tank to represent nature; the environment outside the tank to represent the supernatural – that which is beyond the domain of the natural. Lewis wants to focus on what is required to *explain* certain events that may occur within the tank. I will postpone until later in this chapter my discussion of the problems that attend the notion of supernatural explanation. For now, let us contemplate the metaphysical implications of Lewis's model. In particular, it is important to notice that the interaction between events outside of the fish tank and those within is made possible by the fact that all of the entities involved are of the same sort – they are all *physical* objects possessing *physical* properties, and they are interacting in accordance with *physical* laws. Thus the explosion of a bomb in wartime London compresses air molecules, sending a shock wave toward the fish tank. This shock wave moves the glass of the tank sharply, which creates a compression in the water column, startling the fish.

Lewis would like the interaction of nature with the supernatural to be similar to the way in which forces outside the aquarium may influence events within it. What we need to consider carefully, however, is just how strong an analogy is possible here. We understand, of course, that there are no molecules for God to compress within the supernatural domain; to suppose that there are is to conceive the supernatural in physical terms, with the result that we are no longer conceiving of it as anything distinct in kind from the natural. Thus God cannot influence events in nature by means of the same sort of shock wave that causes the startling of Lewis's fish. To insist on this kind of mechanism for natural–supernatural interaction is to press the analogy too hard. But then, there does not seem to be *any* known mechanism by which God can influence earthly affairs. What sort of force can God exert on natural events? If God is not a physical object, then God cannot exert gravitational force, nor can God radiate any form of electromagnetic field. There is nothing barring anyone from saying that God acts in the natural world by means of a supernatural force of some kind, but if such a force cannot be compared to anything else that we refer to by that designation, then why should we call it a force at all – what warrants our including it under that heading?

Indeed I think we can go even further and make the same observation about the notion of a supernatural cause. We know how one billiard ball can cause another one to move by the transfer of momentum. But if an entity is capable of transferring momentum, then it has mass and is capable of motion; such an entity cannot be a *supernatural* one. On the other hand, if it is a supernatural entity, then it does not have such physical properties as mass, in which case it is incapable of acting on anything by the transfer of momentum. And I think the same thing can be said of any attempt to compare a supernatural cause to a natural one; the supernatural cause will always be lacking some feature that is present in the natural cause and is furthermore essential to it. If any attempt to compare a supernatural cause to a natural one will suffer from this kind of failure of analogy, then we have no business speaking of such things as causes at all. Unless there is some *other* way to lend some content to the conception of a supernatural cause, it thus becomes an empty notion.

Trans-domain Laws

Part of the problem here is that we are able to understand how Lewis's fish are startled because we understand the physical laws that govern the interaction of the tank with its external environment. For there to be analogous interactions between nature and the supernatural, these would have to conform to some form of law. But such laws would have to be distinct from natural law. For if natural–supernatural interactions were subsumable under natural laws, the supernatural becomes nothing more than an extension of the natural. Now there is nothing to prevent us from speculating that the interaction between nature and the supernatural is lawlike – that is, that it takes place under some form of law or another. But we have no idea what any such 'trans-domain' law might be – that is, we do not seem able to form any conception of the sort of law that might govern interactions between the natural and the supernatural domains – since we can only observe the natural side of any supernatural–natural interaction. Nor would we be able to draw on any analogy to natural law in order to illuminate the character of these trans-domain laws. Natural laws always operate in conjunction with physical properties such as mass, momentum, or charge. What could it possibly mean to say, for example, that a law governing the interaction of natural and supernatural entities is *like* a law that governs the interaction of massive bodies, with the exception that – since at least one of the elements of such a law is a supernatural entity and therefore not physical –

it isn't an interaction between massive bodies at all? Once again we see a failure of analogy.

If no understanding of natural law can help us to make sense of the notion of a supernatural law, i.e. one that governs the interaction between nature and the supernatural, there seems to be no utility in speaking of such laws or in speculating about their existence. Indeed the only way we have of conceiving of any causal interaction between events is to think of them as falling under some form of law or regularity; given that we can have no clear conception of what a supernatural regularity might be, we have no business speaking in terms of an interaction between nature and the supernatural at all.

We might also notice here that if we have no clear conception of what sort of laws might govern the operation of supernatural causes, this will be another very strong point of disanalogy to the notion of a physical cause. And once again, we ought to wonder what is left of the notion of a cause, when we speak of supernatural causes, if these do not bear a sufficient analogy to physical causes.

I can imagine a response to this line of argument which insists that to describe God as supernaturally influencing earthly affairs is simply to say that events in nature respond immediately to God's will. If, by the claim that God *causes* x to occur, the critic means only that x occurred because God intended it – i.e. the critic means to invoke a *teleological* conception of 'cause' – I have no objection. Indeed I am in fundamental agreement; I think that the possibility of miracles, and of divine agency generally, depends on whether nature is capable of responding immediately to God's will. However, as I hope to show in Chapter 4, saying that nature immediately reflects God's will does not require us to speak of God as *causing* anything to occur.

Dualism and the Supernatural

We have seen that there are metaphysical problems associated with speaking of causal interaction between nature and the supernatural, at least if this is understood in event-causal terms. We simply lack any conception of how such interactions may take place, and it seems as though any analogy to the ordinary physical interactions that we may experience must fail, if the supernatural is to be understood as a distinct category from the natural. It is interesting to notice that the problem here is the same one that arises in connection with substance dualism, and was forcefully pressed by Princess Elizabeth against Descartes, who wondered how the human mind might bring about motion in the human body:

> For it seems that all determination of movement takes place by the propulsion of the thing moved, by the manner which it is propelled by that which moves it, and by the qualification and shape of the surface of this latter. Contact is required for the first two conditions, and extension for the third. You yourself entirely exclude extension from the notion you have of mind, and a touching seems to me incompatible with an immaterial being. (1952: 270)

Descartes, in his response, appeals to gravity as an example of a force that can move an object without any contact. Elizabeth is not persuaded, and confesses that she finds it easier to think of the mind as being a material entity and possessing extension than she finds it to suppose that it is both immaterial and capable of moving material objects.[6] Descartes admits that he has explained himself badly (1952: 273), but his options are limited; it would seem that the primary alternatives are to abandon a central tenet of his metaphysics and admit that mind is, as Elizabeth suggests, a material entity or to deny, as did the occasionalists, that any causal interaction takes place between mind and body. Descartes attempts to go through the horns of the dilemma and argue that the union of soul with body involves a *kind* of extended entity that is neither present in thought, nor in matter – what appears to be a sort of intermediary kind of existence:

> Since your Highness declares that it is much easier to attribute matter and extension to the soul than to attribute to it the capacity to move a body and to be moved by it [i.e. to be sensuously affected] without being itself material, I beg her to feel

quite free to attribute to the soul this matter and this extension; for that is precisely what we do in apprehending it as united to the body. And after having viewed them in this way, and having experienced the union in herself, it will be easy for her to recognise that the matter she will have thus attributed to this thought is not the same as thought [i.e. not the same as the soul] and that the extension of this matter is of a different nature from any extension that can be attributed to thought. For whereas the extension of matter is determined to a certain location from which it excludes all other corporeal extension, this does not hold of the extension appropriate to thought. (1952: 276)

This, of course, is no help at all. If this intermediary entity does not possess 'a certain location from which it excludes other corporeal existences', then it will still be impossible for it to propel material objects, or to be propelled by them. If I am playing billiards with a cue ball that is capable of inter-permeating the matter of the other balls, I will not be able to get it rolling with my cue stick, and if I could, it would not be capable of setting any of the other balls into motion; it would presumably roll right through them. (All of this presumes, of course, that we can account for how it would even stay on the table.)

All of these same objections can be made against the possibility of divine interaction with nature. Indeed the problems we have discussed above, in connection with the 'open universe' model of the miraculous, are closely associated with the question of mind–body interaction. We can easily imagine Princess Elizabeth articulating objections to Lewis that are parallel to those she offers Descartes. We understand how sound waves might move the wall of Lewis's fish tank and compress the water within, but of course this interaction requires both contact and extension. How can this serve as a model for the interaction between God and nature, given that God is not an extended being and so cannot engage in this kind of contact with a physical object?

The fact that problems associated with God's interaction with nature bear a close resemblance to issues arising in the interaction of mind and body should not surprise us, since God is traditionally conceived as having a spiritual or mental existence, as opposed to a physical one, and I would argue that the difficulties that an account of supernatural causation faces are the very same ones that are encountered by the substance dualist. This is an important realization, for it points the way toward progress in our future discussions of the relation between God and the natural world; what it suggests is that we can learn much from parallel discussions in the philosophy of mind, where these concern the nature of mind and its relation to the physical.

Chapter 3

Supernatural Explanation

We are exploring some of the difficulties involved in a supernaturalistic conception of miracles, according to which a miracle is thought to be the effect of a supernatural cause. In the last chapter we observed some difficulties with the very notion of a supernatural cause. The supernaturalist appears to conceive of such causes as closely analogous to natural causes. But there does not appear to be any analogy possible here. Natural causes are understood as involving physical properties. But a supernatural cause cannot possess any physical, or natural, properties without becoming a *natural* cause. Yet if a supernatural cause is conceived as being too dissimilar to natural causes, we are right to wonder what justifies thinking of them as causes at all.

We also observed that there are difficulties in explaining how it is that supernatural entities can interact causally with objects in nature. Part of the problem here is that natural causes operate in accordance with natural laws. But it does not seem to be possible to obtain any very clear idea of what sort of law would govern interactions between nature and the supernatural.

I have been postponing discussion of an important possibility, which is that we may be entitled to say that an event has a supernatural cause when it is possible to give a supernatural explanation for it. The supernaturalist may hope to appeal to this possibility to overcome some of the epistemic problems that she has encountered so far. Supposing that an anomaly occurs, we may have reason to think it is supernaturally caused when we are able to provide a supernatural explanation for it. Furthermore, if we can give a clear account of what a supernatural explanation would be, this might help us to see more clearly what is meant by a supernatural cause. The present chapter will be concerned primarily with examining the notion of a supernatural explanation.

I have also been postponing another discussion, which will revolve around the possibility that, in saying a miracle is caused by God, we merely wish to say that it expresses God's agency – that it is an action on God's part. This possibility will begin to receive some discussion in this chapter, though I will wait until Chapter 4 before making my case that, in identifying something as an action on the part of God, we need not say that God caused it to occur.

Thus I turn now to a discussion of the notion of a *supernatural explanation*, which is another key component of supernaturalism. After all, the whole point of saying that a miracle is an event that violates natural law, or somehow fails to have a natural explanation, is to make it the occasion for an explanation that is supernatural. I will begin by examining Patrick Nowell-Smith's naturalistic attack on the notion of a supernatural explanation. Nowell-Smith argues that any adequate explanation must be testable, being capable of yielding true predictions, but that any testable explanation would be consistent with the methods of the natural sciences, and so would fail to be distinctively supernatural. Nowell-Smith may be understood as offering a challenge: to give an explanation that is at once testable, and at the same time supernatural. I will consider the response of Paul Dietl, who attempts to answer Nowell-Smith's challenge. Dietl suggests that miracles might occur under circumstances in which they may give us true predictions, and so they offer us the chance to give testable explanations for them, but that these explanations will be distinctively supernatural.

Before I discuss Dietl's response I will point out an important feature of his defense, which is that the sort of explanation he has in mind appears to be a teleological one. Thus he appears to be shifting ground from the kind of supernaturalistic account we have been considering up until now. Then I will try to show that Dietl is partly right in his response. There may be miracles that can receive the sort of explanation that Dietl proposes; nevertheless, he fails to meet Nowell-Smith's challenge: there is nothing in Dietl's explanations that is distinctively supernatural. Furthermore, I will argue that it is wrong to say that all of the miracles that theistic religion may want to countenance can receive the sort of explanation that Dietl has in mind.

Nowell-Smith and Predictive Expansion

One of the most powerful criticisms that has been made of the appeal to supernatural explanation – as this is understood in terms of the 'open universe' model, as we referred to it in the last chapter – is due to Patrick Nowell-Smith. Nowell-Smith argues that any genuine explanation must be capable of *predictive expansion*; that is, it must be based on a hypothesis that, in virtue of its ability to generate true predictions, would be testable. For example, suppose we want to explain how a fire was started; we explain this by saying that someone dropped a lighted match onto some dry leaves. If this is a good explanation for how the fire started, then it must, on Nowell-Smith's view, make a prediction possible: In this example, we would predict that the next time someone drops a match onto dry leaves in relevantly similar circumstances, a fire will start – and of course we can always perform the experiment to see if this hypothesis is correct.

Nowell-Smith notes that such predictions are made possible by the fact that explanations generally depend on laws. It is this fact, on his view, that makes it possible for an explanation to say *how* its explanandum comes about. In the example above, our ability to predict that a fire will start when a lighted match is dropped onto dry leaves is based, in a fairly obvious way, on a generalization: 'When a lighted match is dropped onto dry leaves, a fire will start.'

Now it is easy to imagine an objection here, which is that this is not really a *law*, in the sense in which that term might be used in physics. Although we can say something about *how* the fire started – a lighted match was dropped onto dry leaves – nothing has been said so far about *how* a lighted match is able to do this, though of course a more fundamental physical explanation is possible here, in terms of molecular motion, heat of activation, and so forth. Nevertheless the generalization as it stands is an empirical one – it specifies an observable antecedent condition (a lighted match is dropped onto dry leaves) together with an observable consequence (a fire will start); this is all we need for our prediction, and to make the explanation testable.

Nowell-Smith insists that, to the extent that any purported super-natural explanation is testable, and therefore actually has explan-atory power, it ought to be counted as a *natural* explanation. In this case it would be 'nothing but a new field for scientific inquiry, a field as different from physics as physics is from psychology, but not differing in principle or requiring any non-scientific method' (1955: 253). To the extent that theology concerns itself with such explanations, it qualifies as a branch of the natural sciences. If Nowell-Smith is right about this, then any attempt at providing a supernatural explanation for some phenomenon must fail; it will either fail to be an adequate explanation at all, or, to the extent that it is adequate, will not differ substantially from a natural explana-tion. Interestingly, this would seem to leave open the possibility that some phenomena might be explained by reference to *God.* But the supernatural character of this explanation evaporates.

It is important to notice that Nowell-Smith appears to be using the term 'law' quite broadly, if he means for it to encompass the method of any of the natural sciences. Biology and psychology do not generally appeal to what we might call laws, if the model for a law is provided by physics; they draw on generalizations of a somewhat rougher sort. Nevertheless even a rough generalization can yield a prediction. It will be important to notice that it is enough for Nowell-Smith's purposes that an explanation be sup-ported by *some* sort of generalization, one that is sufficient to yield at least a vague prediction. As an example of what I mean by a 'vague' prediction, we may consider the possibility that an adequate explanation might facilitate the judgement that some event is likely, though not certain, to occur – or that at least, the adequacy of the explanation allows us to say that it is *more* likely to occur than otherwise would be the case. Thus, for example, if I can explain Mildred's devotion to a life of violent crime by saying that she was deprived of affection as a child, it need not be the case that every child so deprived will take up a life of violent crime. It need only be the case, at most, that such children are more likely to do so than other children.

Nowell-Smith's remarks were made in response to an article by Arnold Lunn in which Lunn, himself responding to an article by Homer Dubbs (1950), attempted to argue that miracles are just as lawful as natural events – and what he had in mind was that they conform to supernatural laws. Lunn wrote:

> Everything which happens, happens in accordance with law but not necessarily in accordance with natural law. The supernatural also has its laws. A cricket ball is hit into the air, and falls toward the ground under the law of gravity. A fieldsman catches the ball and the further fall is averted. The law of gravity is not violated but its consequences have been modified by human will. When God works a miracle he does not violate the laws of nature but modifies some of the normal effects of those laws by a process analogous to that by which the human will influences nature. (1950: 241)

Lunn does not explain what he means by a supernatural law. He does say that divine agency operates in a way similar to human agency, and it is possible that he supposes human agency to be supernatural;[1] otherwise, as Nowell-Smith points out, the analogy has no point (1955: 246). Unfortunately Lunn does not elaborate on this issue; rather, he proceeds to make an implicit distinction between the manner in which natural and supernatural agency take place, since he holds that a miracle is 'inexplicable as the effect of natural agents and must therefore be ascribed to supernatural agents' (1950: 242). Let us notice, however, that whatever Lunn has in mind, in speaking of supernatural laws or supernatural explanation, he seems to want to include teleological elements; that is, the concept of *agency* seems to form an important part of his thinking,[2] though it is not clear just how the comparison of supernatural causes to human agency is supposed to fit in, and particularly how the human will is supposed to act to modify the normal effects of the laws of nature, as he puts it. We may be forgiven, perhaps, for supposing that Lunn's supernaturalism conflates teleological considerations with the sort of causal concerns that are the primary focus of the natural sciences.

Lunn then commences to describe the natural universe as open to influences originating from outside of it, attempting to draw an analogy between the supernatural forces he thinks operate on nature from the outside, and the purely natural forces that operate within it:

> The determination to regard the natural order as a closed system is a dogma which is completely sterilising in its influence on research. An analogous dogma would have been equally fatal to astronomical research. If Leverrier for instance had assumed that the planetary order was a closed system, he would never have discovered Neptune. This unknown planet was causing 'perturbations' of the planetary movements inexplicable in terms of the planets that were known. Miracles might be defined as 'perturbations' inexplicable in terms of known natural forces. Now if Leverrier had argued like Professor Dubs he would have said:
>
>> these perturbations are very puzzling but no doubt the astronomy of the future will reconcile these perturbations with the planets as known to us. There is not the slightest reason to postulate an unknown planet. The belief in undiscovered planets can without difficulty be dismissed as due to misunderstanding myth or mistake. (1950: 243)

Neptune was discovered because of perturbations in the orbit of Uranus. Leverrier found Neptune by looking for the cause of these perturbations, but of course the interaction between these two planets is gravitational, and so conforms to natural law. Miracles, on Lunn's view, are lawful, but the laws involved are supernatural laws, and it is significant that his analogy draws on a comparison of such laws to the laws governing the irregularities in the orbit of Uranus, i.e. gravity and angular momentum. The conception of supernatural causation to which he appears to be appealing is thus analogous to the kind of causal influence that Neptune exerts on Uranus, i.e. it is analogous to *physical* causation. This is the conception of supernatural causation that Nowell-Smith wants to criticize; he hopes to undermine the idea that there is a lawlike interaction between supernatural causes and natural effects that is analogous to the interactions that take place among natural objects, in accordance with natural laws.

Taking on Lunn's conception of a supernatural law, Nowell-Smith argues that a law must satisfy three important criteria. He thinks that any law that satisfied these criteria would be a *natural* law, and so he challenges Lunn to show how supernatural laws might do this, while still maintaining the contrast between the supernatural and the natural:

> It might be argued that God's interventions are indeed 'lawful'; but that they proceed according to laws which are not 'natural laws'; but at this point the difference between a 'natural' and a 'supernatural' law cries out for explanation . . . If it is a law, it must (a) be based on evidence, (b) be of a general type, 'Under such and such conditions, so and so will happen'; (c) be capable of testing in experience. And if it conforms to this specification, how does it differ from a natural law? (1955: 249)

We have no direct experience of anything beyond nature; the very best we can do is make inferences about what lies beyond nature that are based on what we can observe. Considering Nowell-Smith's three criteria, then, (a) the only evidence for any law that we could collect would be empirical evidence. The law must be testable in experience (c), which means that it must have empirical consequences. And we are only capable of testing it if these consequences have antecedent conditions that are themselves accessible to our experience; in this case, (b) the law will have the form 'Under such and such conditions, so and so will happen', as Nowell-Smith says it must, but the antecedent and consequent conditions are both empirical. Any such law would be a natural law, a generalization regarding what is observed (that is, nature) rather than what is unobservable (the supernatural).

Nowell-Smith's point about supernatural law carries over to the closely related notion of a supernatural explanation:

Any explanation . . . must be capable of application to new phenomena. Now, Mr. Lunn's explanations are inevitably ex post facto; we can only recognize a miracle after it has occurred . . . My argument is not intended to show that Mr. Lunn's hypothesis is false; it is intended to show that it is not an hypothesis at all. It is as if one were to say: 'Certain events in the past were caused by boojums; but I cannot tell you on what principles boojums operate or what they will do in the future; my hypothesis inevitably involves this consequence.' If anyone said this, we should have to treat his phrase 'caused by boojums' as simply a special way of describing the phenomena, moreover in a misleading way, since it looks like an explanatory hypothesis. But in fact it is not. (1955: 250)

Suppose we are to say that the occurrence of a miracle is to be *explained* by saying that it was caused by God. The problem, as Nowell-Smith sees it, is that we can impute divine causality to an event in nature only after the fact, i.e. the supposed hypothesis that God is the cause of the event is incapable of generating any predictions about the future, and his reasoning appears to be that we simply cannot predict the occurrence of a miracle. It therefore becomes misleading to say that we can explain an event as being caused by God, since we appear to be offering an explanatory hypothesis when in fact we are not.

It will help to apply Nowell-Smith's argument to an example. Suppose a heavy anvil made of iron levitates some three feet above the ground. Being unable to find any natural cause for the phenomenon, the apologist claims that it was God who caused the anvil to levitate, and that this *explains* its levitation. But we will be in one of two situations here. (1) We find that we are unable to say what the circumstances are in which God may be expected to perform such levitations. According to Nowell-Smith, this means that 'God caused the anvil to levitate' is not an explanation for the levitation of the anvil. Notice the contrast to a scientific explanation, e.g. 'A large magnet caused the anvil to lift off the ground.' This has explanatory value because it is testable; if we bring such a magnet near the anvil at a later date, the anvil will levitate once again.

It seems likely that in this case, Nowell-Smith would be likely to say that the claim that God caused the anvil to levitate, since it does not offer any real explanation for the movement of the anvil, seems to be tantamount to admitting that *we have no idea* what caused the anvil to levitate.

Alternatively, (2) suppose we *are* able predictively to expand our explanation, so that we are in a position to say when and where God will cause an object like an anvil to levitate. In order to predict the levitation of an anvil, there would have to be some observable circumstance which would signal that the anvil is about to be raised. (Perhaps we hear a booming voice announce the imminent raising of the anvil.) In this case, according to Nowell-Smith, there would no longer be any reason to call the explanation 'supernatural'. It would seem to be an instance of *natural* explanation, and falls under the scope of the scientific method.

We should not suppose that the problem with predictive expansion, as it pertains to purported supernatural explanations, lies merely in the fact that God, as a supernatural cause, is in principle unobservable. The natural sciences regularly appeal to the existence of unobservable entities such as electrons, magnetic fields, and black holes; perhaps the apologist conceives her own appeal as having a similar character (Geivett 1997: 183). These things, one may argue, may be known only through their observable effects. But the causal properties of such natural entities as electrons and magnetic fields are analogous to those of entities that *are* observable. The principles by which they operate are natural principles, of the same kind as those by which observable entities operate. This is what entitles us to refer to electrons and black holes as natural entities. These properties may be described in terms of regularities that are observable, which means that entities like electrons and magnetic fields may play a role in theories that have predictive power. Furthermore, even though we may not be able to observe directly the occurrence of some quantum event, we can predict the occurrence of such events by reference to circumstances that are observable. Consider, for example, a strange quark, which is (as far as I know) a subatomic particle that is, in principle, not directly observable, and can be known only from its effects. Nevertheless we can predict what such a quark will do, because strange quarks – while they cannot themselves be observed – are produced under circumstances that *are* observable. Thus suppose some effect *e* of a strange quark, whatever that might be; if our ability to predict *e* depended only on our ability to observe the quark that produces it, we would be unable to do so. However, we know – or perhaps I should say, particle physicists know – that such quarks are produced under a certain set of circumstances by the collision of particular sorts of particles, and that such collisions come about under some particular set of observable circumstances *c*; *c* thus becomes a predictor for *e*. Thus explanations by reference to strange quarks are capable of predictive expansion *despite* the fact that such quarks are not directly observable. However, there does not seem to be any similar set of observable circumstances that will allow us to predict a miracle.

The important question here is just how close the apologist wants the analogy to be between God and the unobserved entities of physical theory such as electrons, quarks, and magnetic fields. If the analogy is too close, it becomes difficult to say why God should not be thought of as a physical entity. God, viewed as the cause of a miracle, would then fail to be different in any important respect from a physical object. Supernatural causes, on this view, become *natural* causes. Yet the more strongly we insist on God being a supernatural entity, the less ground we have for any analogy between explanations by reference to divine agency, and physical causation or physical explanation.

Perhaps one might say that the entities involved in supernatural causation are simply those that are in principle unobservable, so that 'supernatural' just means 'natural but in principle unobservable'. In this case God qualifies as a supernatural cause – but so do quarks and electrons. This is a possible view, of course, but one that I think will not appeal to mainstream Christian theology, which tends to interpret passages such as John 4.24, for example, as insisting that 'God is spirit' (*pneuma*); similarly 2 Corinthians 3.17 ('Now the Lord is the Spirit . . . '). Furthermore Roman Catholic doctrine, at least, insists on the absolute simplicity of God, which is taken to imply that 'God is pure spirit . . . neither a body nor a composition of body and spirit'; while the Old Testament represents God anthropomorphically, 'it expresses God's spirituality by representing Him as supreme over matter and as the ruler of matter' (Ott 1955: 31).

Nowell-Smith concludes:

> Let him consider the meaning of the word 'explanation' and let him ask himself whether this notion or hypothesis is capable of predictive expansion. And then let him ask himself whether such an explanation would not be natural, in whatever terms it was couched, and how the notion of 'the supernatural' could play any part in it . . .
>
> The supernatural is either so different from the natural that we are unable to investigate it at all or it is not. If it is not, then it can hardly have the momentous significance that Mr. Lunn claims for it; and if it is it cannot be invoked as an explanation for the unusual. (1955: 253)

According to Nowell-Smith, the apologist who wishes to speak in terms of supernatural causes and supernatural explanations faces a dilemma. Either her supposed supernatural explanations are capable of predictive expansion, in which case they are not supernatural explanations at all but natural ones, or they fail to have any explanatory force at all. Thus Nowell-Smith offers a challenge to the supernaturalist, and that is to show how a supernatural explanation really can succeed in having real explanatory force, and yet be distinctively *supernatural*, that is, to show that this is not the sort of explanation that is consistent with the methods of the natural sciences.

Do Explanations Always Rely on Laws?

The most obvious response that might be made to Nowell-Smith's challenge is to deny that adequate explanations really do require any reference to laws. While it seems hard to deny that scientific explanations rest for their cogency on various kinds of laws, this is not obviously true of *teleological* explanations. Thus Richard Taylor argues:

> There is, to be sure, a sense of 'explanation' much in vogue according to which teleological explanations, even in the realm of human behavior, are not real explanations, or are at least dubious as such. According to this interpretation, something is alleged to be 'explained' only if it was *predictable*, that is, only if there is some general *law* from which, together with certain data consisting of the observable occurrences of other things, the thing in question could have been predicted. Now it is doubtful whether the purposeful behavior of men, or at least of individuals, is always explicable in that sense. Apart from the behavior of fairly large groups of men in certain situations having a common pattern, there seem to be no such laws. If there are, they certainly are not known. There are, for example, no laws in terms of which the purposeful behavior of an individual man from one moment to the next can be predicted. (1966: 218ff., original emphasis)

Taylor argues that it is doubtful that there could even *be* such laws predicting the behavior of individual human beings, since humans are capable of employing any number of *means* to accomplish some particular end. Thus suppose that I manage to offend a relative by making an insensitive remark of some kind. I cannot predict that she will seek revenge, and even if she tells me that she plans to do so, I cannot (alas) predict when, where, or how it will manifest itself. Yet once she exacts her comeuppance, there seems little question that her action can be explained by reference to her intention to avenge herself for having been slighted by me.

While Taylor may be right to say that the particular actions of individual human beings are difficult to predict with any precision, and that human behavior does not, at least to the best of our knowledge, conform to any well-formed laws, it does seem to me that we can give at least rough predictions of what a particular human being will do, and that he is overstating the case for the unpredictability of human action. To borrow an example from Hume:

A prisoner knows that he is better off trying to cut through the bars of his cell than to try to talk his guard into letting him out – which is to say that, in some instances at least, we can make predictions regarding human behavior that are just as reliable as the predictions we would make in regard to the physical characteristics of iron bars and the like.

Still, Taylor seems to have a point. It seems possible that the value of intentional explanations does not generally rely on our ability to make predictions, even though an agent may act in an utterly unpredictable way, and that when she does, her action may be explained by reference to her intention. Suppose that when I go for my morning coffee, the person who makes it for me – who happens to own the shop – unexpectedly announces that my coffee will be free this morning. I might never have predicted this; indeed I would have predicted *against* it, had I been asked in advance. Yet I can imagine someone wanting to say that we *explain* what she has done by saying that she gave me the coffee intentionally, particularly if we can fill this out by specifying her motive, e.g. that she has taken a liking to me or feels sorry for me, etc. Certainly there is some sense in which telling such a story makes her action intelligible in a way that it would not be otherwise.

Of course we might say that the value of describing her action as intentional in this way facilitates at least a rough prediction about what she may do in the future; we assess the odds of her giving other things away as being slightly higher than they are for other shopkeepers. Yet it seems wrong to say, in the event that this prediction is not borne out, that this somehow undermines the elucidatory character of saying that she gave me the coffee on purpose. If this is true, then the criteria for adequacy in a teleological explanation seem to be quite different, at least in this one respect, from those that apply to the sort of explanation favored by the natural sciences. It is possible that there is no place for such explanations in the physical sciences. But it does not follow from this that they can have no value at all.

What is the significance of this for the supernaturalist? Suppose that something completely unexpected occurs. A child, thought to be terminally ill, suddenly recovers; a tumor in her brain has disappeared overnight. We are confronted with an anomaly. The supernaturalist wants to say that this event has a supernatural explanation, and that this provides the basis for saying that it has a supernatural cause.

In the spirit of Nowell-Smith, let us ask whether this is any different from saying that the cure was due to the influence of boojums. (Let us suppose for the moment that this is *not* intended to provide a teleological explanation for the cure.) Nowell-Smith, of course, would say that this is no explanation at all, primarily because we cannot predict what effects will arise from the causal influence of boojums. Saying that the cure was due to boojums seems no better than simply describing it as an anomaly.

Now let us add the stipulation that boojums are, after all, *persons*, and that we intend, by explaining the cure as the activity of boojums, to provide a teleological explanation for it. This does not seem to help in the slightest. But what is the problem here? Is it that we have no idea what sort of thing boojums can be expected to do? If we say this, we appear to be drawing back into a predictability criterion for the adequacy of intentional explanations. And suppose we add to our explanation the information that boojums are some sort of benign spirit, so that we can say that the child's cure is compatible with our understanding of the nature of boojums. But this doesn't seem to help at all. The 'explanation' in this case is still vacuous.

But suppose now that we attribute the child's cure to divine agency. Surely we can do this despite acknowledging that the cure was entirely unpredictable. I have the very strong intuition, however, that it really *means something* to attribute the cure to God where it means nothing to say that it is the work of boojums, even if we try to construe this in terms of 'boojum agency'. But why is this? Surely it is, at least in part, because when we attribute the cure to God, we place it against the background of a religious view of the world, and we open up the possibility of incorporating it into a theistic religious practice. We may light a candle or offer thanks and praise to God; we might make the child's return to health the subject of a vow. The child herself may be moved, later in life, to take up holy orders. All of this means seeing a kind of significance in our description of God as curing the child that is not present when we attribute it to boojums.

Two observations now force themselves upon us. First, it seems evident that the kind of explanation we are offering here is quite different from the sort that is the stock in trade of the physical scientist. There is a very great deal that can be said about this, and I will not explore the matter in detail here. The most obvious point is that it involves no commitment in regard to predictability. I can imagine, however, someone wanting to say more – wanting to say, for example, that God's curing the child entails an obligation on the part of the child, or those who care for her, to thank God, at the very least, or to perform some other religiously significant observance. And of course scientific discoveries never entail, on their own, the appropriacy of any particular human response. In this case, when we say that God cured the child, we elucidate the child's curing – we make it intelligible – by showing what its place is within the context of theistic religion. And here we begin to give an answer to the question: What do we add to an anomaly by attributing it to divine agency? We show its significance to theistic religious practice.

The second observation is this: Suppose we agree that we have explained the child's cure when we say this is something that God has done. Is this of any help to the supernaturalist? Perhaps it is – if it follows from the fact that God does x that God causes x to occur. However, as I hope to show in Chapter 4, it does not. I do not, therefore, see that this kind of explanation can offer any solace to supernaturalism as we have understood it here.[3]

Paul Dietl's Response to Nowell-Smith's Challenge

We have considered Nowell-Smith's argument against the conception of a supernatural law, and against the possibility of giving a supernatural explanation for any natural event; his view is that supposed supernatural explanations fail to have any real explanatory value because they are not capable of giving us predictions. By the same token, should such explanations be capable of predictive expansion, they qualify as *natural* explanations.

Paul Dietl takes up Nowell-Smith's challenge to show how we can explain the occurrence of a miracle, and yet maintain that the explanation is a supernatural one, where it is possible to maintain a real contrast between the supernatural and the natural – that is, where the supernatural is *not* conceived as falling under the method of the natural sciences. He believes that when we explain a miracle by reference to divine agency, the explanation we give may be capable of predictive expansion, but he denies that such an explanation involves any reference to laws.

Dietl notices that some of the miracles reported in the Bible are associated with prophets who are able to perform miracles on multiple occasions. Consider the Old Testament story of the prophet Elijah calling fire down from the sky to incinerate a bull. After having a bull placed on an altar, Elijah challenges the priests of Baal to call on their god to send fire down from heaven to burn the bull as a sacrifice. After they fail to do so, Elijah, with great confidence, has wood placed around the bull and water poured around the altar in trenches; following Elijah's entreaty, 'the fire of the Lord fell and burned up the sacrifice, the wood, the stones and the soil, and even licked up the water in the trench' (1 Kings 18.38 NIV).

Dietl argues that the setting of Elijah's miracle gives us 'about as artificial a setting as any laboratory affords' (1968: 131). He continues:

> The account also involves a random sampling of the material to be set on fire, a prediction that one pile will burn up and one will not, a prediction as to when the fire will start, and twelve barrels of precaution against earthly independent variables. There is obviously nothing wrong with applying somewhat sophisticated experimental design to miracles.

Indeed he suggests that, in principle, the working of miracles is quite testable, and he constructs an example of how such testing might be done, with an imaginary prophet being asked to perform miracles chosen at random by rolling a set of dice. Our prediction about what will happen, when we ask the prophet to perform a miracle, is not made possible by a law; 'what is needed,' Dietl says, 'is not a law but an understanding that can grasp the request and then bring it about that a physical law be broken' (1968: 132). Dietl denies that any natural law can be at work here:

> No natural law will do because only vehicles of thought could function as the natural *explanans* and no such vehicle is necessary. There would have to be one law connecting the acoustics of English with general law breaking, another for French, and so on indefinitely – and when the prophet asks that whatever miracle turns up on the dice be performed and then goes to sleep before the dice are thrown there just is not anything left except his request as understood. (1968: 132)

The argument seems to be that it is sufficient, in order to explain the occurrence of the miracle, to refer to an understanding that is capable of comprehending the prophet's request and then granting it. There is no need to look for a physical mechanism; indeed this would be a daunting task, since we would have to find one that would be equally responsive to the physical properties of a request made in an indefinite number of ways and in any possible language.

Analysis of Dietl's Response

There are a couple of things we ought to notice about the strategy Dietl employs in his attempt to rebut Nowell-Smith. First, he seems to understand supernatural explanations as a species of *personal* explanation; that is, the sort of explanation he offers is one that we have been referring to as intentional or teleological. It is not uncommon to defend the conception of supernatural explanation as a species of personal explanation.[4] However, the fact that Dietl is appealing to the principles of personal explanation means he has shifted ground in regard to the position of Mr Lunn, who was the original target of Nowell-Smith's criticism. Lunn was happy to embrace the notion of a supernatural law, apparently intending a close analogy to the laws of nature; Dietl rejects such a stance. It is interesting, too, that Dietl accepts Nowell-Smith's challenge to show how an explanation in terms of supernatural causes may be capable of predictive expansion; he does not contest Nowell-Smith's claim that an adequate explanation must be testable in this way, and we ought to suspect that in this regard he may have conceded too much to Nowell-Smith.

The dispute between Dietl and Nowell-Smith thus centers on whether supernatural explanations, having been shown to be testable, at least in principle, have been reduced to a species of *natural* explanation and therefore fall under the domain of the natural sciences, as Nowell-Smith insists. Dietl wants to argue that such explanations remain properly supernatural.

To use Dietl's example of Elijah calling down fire from the sky, let us notice that there is a sense in which we can, and a sense in which we cannot, explain how the fire comes from the sky. To the question, 'How did the fire come from the sky?' we might answer, 'Because Elijah called upon God to send it, and God generally accedes to Elijah's requests'. We would be hard-pressed to deny that this response has explanatory value. Yet of course we are still, in another sense, quite in the dark as to how fire came from the sky, if the question is directed at making clear the *mechanism* that made this possible, i.e. when it comes to asking *how* God managed it. As far as this sort of explanation goes, the matter remains a mystery.

Problems with Dietl's Response

It seems to me that Dietl has failed to answer Nowell-Smith's challenge. He has found an instance in which we might explain the occurrence of a miracle as being a response to a request, and his explanation possesses real explanatory force in virtue of being predictively expandable. The kind of explanatory force it possesses appears to be the same sort that is the stock in trade of the natural sciences. However, he has failed to show that the explanation that is involved is something that does not conform to the methods of the natural sciences. There is, in short, nothing distinctively *supernatural* about the explanation that he offers.

Dietl is correct in saying that no law allows us to predict when and where the fire will strike, when Elijah petitions God to send it down to the altar on Mount Carmel. But what makes this prediction possible is that we know something about Elijah's history, and understand that the requests he makes of God are usually answered.[5] This, of course, is a generalization, and without it we would have no way of knowing what will happen when Elijah calls for the fire. That is, Elijah's history seems to enable a generalization having the form, 'When Elijah calls on God to bring about x, then x occurs'. This is not a law, if the notion of 'law' is the one used in physics and chemistry.[6] But it is a generalization nevertheless, and without it, our prediction that fire will come down from the sky, when Elijah asks God to send it, would not be possible. By contrast, suppose that *I* call for God to send down fire from heaven. No one in their right mind would expect the fire to come. This is because, unlike Elijah, I have no record of success with such requests. There is no evidence for the truth of the generalization 'When Corner asks God to bring about x, then x occurs'.

Now consider the generalization that makes prediction possible in the case of Elijah. It has the form (as Nowell-Smith would say) 'Under such and such conditions, so and so will happen'; when Elijah asks God to bring about x, then x occurs. But notice that both the antecedent and the consequent conditions are *empirical* conditions – e.g. in the instance in which Elijah calls for the fire, both the request, and the fire, are observable. If our generalization were not based on observable conditions, no prediction would be possible.

Nowell-Smith's claim was that any adequate explanation would have to enable predictions, and in order to do this it would have to involve some form of law. But Nowell-Smith's argument was that if it satisfied these conditions, it would be a natural explanation, i.e. it would be consistent with naturalism. Dietl, citing the case of Elijah, has found a situation in which the occurrence of a miracle conforms to a hypothesis which is capable of predictive expansion – 'When Elijah petitions God for x, x usually occurs' – and while it does not seem to appeal to what we would ordinarily call a *law*, in the sense of a law of physics, it does seem to involve a generalization; given the rather loose conception of 'law' that Nowell-Smith seems to be invoking, this seems consistent with his account of explanatory adequacy. But it is also hard to see what is supernatural about the sort of explanation that Dietl thinks is at work here.

Given that it is empirically testable, why should we not take it as falling under the method of the natural sciences?

One might argue that Dietl's explanation is a supernatural one because of its explanandum; what is purportedly being explained is a violation of natural law. Yet if what we have observed in Chapter 1 is correct, it does not seem to be possible to draw any conclusions about the supernatural from the occurrence of a purported violation. But interestingly, Dietl argues that this explanation is a supernatural one in virtue of its explanans: 'An understanding physical law breaker,' he avers, 'is a supernatural being' (1968: 132). The miracle is explained by reference to God, who, being capable of violating a natural law, is a supernatural rather than a natural entity.

Now once again, we should notice that in one sense this explains the appearance of Elijah's fire, and in another it does not. One may say that the explanation for why the fire came down out of the sky is that Elijah asked God to send it, and God possesses an understanding capable of grasping such a request and granting it. But of course what is left unexplained is *how God does it,* where this would mean saying something about the mechanics of the event, or the means God employed to bring it about. How God, or anyone else, can bring it about that fire comes from the sky is something that remains a mystery. So Dietl's attempt to give a supernatural explanation for the event gives us no more than the natural sciences can in this respect.

We have already considered, in Chapter 1, the difficulties that come with speaking of an anomaly as a violation of the laws of nature. Let us waive our objections for the moment; perhaps we can, for this discussion, suppose 'violation' to be synonymous with 'anomaly'. It is difficult to see how the ability to violate a natural law must point to God's character *qua supernatural* entity. It seems to me that the ability to violate natural law could just as easily be attributed to a *natural* agent. Suppose I ask my neighbor Harry to bring fire down from the sky. 'Harry, I beseech thee, bring fire from the sky.' 'Done,' says Harry, and there is the fire. Assuming (with Dietl) that the bringing of fire from the sky qualifies as a violation of physical law, Harry now counts as a supernatural being on Dietl's criterion; he possesses an understanding capable of grasping a request, and then, in response, violating a natural law. The problem is that supernatural entities are generally thought to be unobservable. Yet here is Harry, standing in front of my house, giving every appearance of being a *natural* agent who is capable of violating natural law. So, contrary to Dietl's assertion, what makes God a supernatural agent – if God's sending fire from the sky is an instance of supernatural agency – does not seem to have much to do with God's ability to violate natural laws. The reference to a violation captures nothing of the supernatural.

One possibility is that we should say that God is a supernatural being by virtue of being a *non-embodied agent*.[7] I have no objection to the use of 'supernatural' to describe non-embodied agents; indeed this seems to reflect popular usage, e.g. in works of fiction,[8] where non-embodied entities such as ghosts are often counted as supernatural.[9] I am not, of course, admitting that any such entities exist, but the notion of non-embodied agency appears to be a cogent one – at least where the actions of such an agent are observable. Now this might be one way of accounting for the supernatural element in events like God's sending down fire from heaven in response to Elijah's request; the agent to whom the petition is addressed is a supernatural being, not because that agent violates natural law, but because that agent is in principle unobservable.

Nevertheless we should notice that there is still nothing here that is inconsistent with the method of the natural sciences, as long as our explanations remain capable of predictive expansion. It is conceivable, for example, that the natural universe possesses fundamental properties that can only be described in teleological terms; perhaps it is governed by some sort of Stoic *logos*, where this is understood in immanent rather than transcendent terms. Such a hypothesis is quite compatible with naturalism. In this case our teleological explanations would not appear to be different in kind from explanations that refer to other unobservables such as quarks.[10] I conclude, then, that Dietl has failed to show that there is anything especially supernatural about his explanation for Elijah's summoning of the fire; there is nothing here to suggest that such an explanation does not fall under the umbrella of the natural sciences.

It seems to me that Dietl was misguided in taking up Nowell-

Smith's challenge to show that supernatural explanations may be capable of predictive expansion. In the first place, he failed to show that the explanation he wanted to offer really was a *supernatural* one. But in addition, and quite ironically, while his interest was to show that there was a species of explanation that is uniquely theological, he wound up missing what is distinctive about our references to divine agency – namely, the particular role that these references play in the practice of theistic religion. Unlike scientific explanations, their primary function is not that of prediction.

Divine Agency in Religious Practice

The supernaturalist wants to show that the natural sciences require supplementation of some kind – that the natural sciences, once they have said everything they have to say, have left important things *unsaid.* If our talk about God hopes to complete the narrative, and if this means making the world intelligible in a way that the natural sciences cannot, then it must proceed either (a) by denying that its primary purpose is to provide explanations, or (b) articulating a strategy of explanation that is genuinely different in its method from that employed by the natural sciences.

I am arguing that theology is not confined to giving the sort of explanation that we find in the natural sciences, and I think we ought to notice something quite important, which is that not all of the miracles in the Bible – nor even all of the miracles that might be thought to occur since biblical times – can be explained in anything remotely resembling the manner in which the natural sciences illuminate their explananda. First, it is important to notice that the sort of treatment Dietl gives to the miracles of Elijah is not one that will apply to all of the miracles of the Bible. Dietl, in his attempt to meet Nowell-Smith's challenge and provide an example of a miracle-explanation that was capable of predictive expansion, trained his focus on prophets who were capable of repeated miracles – Elijah, and the prophet in Dietl's imaginary example. If our explanations of such phenomena really are capable of predictive expansion, it is only in virtue of the fact that these prophets are able to call for miracles in a reliable way. To be sure, the case of Elijah is not an isolated one; in addition to Elijah, Elisha is reported to have worked a good many miracles, and Moses is another obvious example. In the New Testament, however, things are somewhat different.[11] If one were to make the claim that the miracles of the Bible are generally foreseeable, the resurrection of Jesus is a notable exception. As the events surrounding the resurrection are reported in the New Testament, it is clear that no one expected Jesus to come back to life after being crucified. Yet Christians want to say that this was an expression of divine agency, and they commonly wish, as well, to say that it is important to know *why* the resurrection took place, i.e. what its significance is to human life. This appears to require a kind of explanation. But the principles of Dietl's 'explanatory supernaturalism' are much too narrow to accommodate this interest.

We ought also to consider the fact that many people would like to say that miracles continue to occur, despite the fact that there are no longer any miracle workers like Elijah and Moses present to request them. We may want to say that the sick child in our earlier example was cured in response to her father's prayers. Her father calls it a miracle, and the Vatican begins an investigation. Yet as we have already observed, nothing could be more clear than that the healing of the child was not predictable. It is possible that her father held a conviction that she would be healed, but there is no rational basis for this belief. One might say that a prediction is possible *in principle* given the assumption that healings will occur whenever God wills them. But given the fact that there are no empirical criteria by which we can determine when God can be expected to heal someone, then as far as predictions are concerned, this seems no better than saying that sometimes people are healed of their diseases, and sometimes they are not.

Of course the obvious point here is that very commonly, people pray to be healed and they are not healed, and so their requests of God go unfulfilled; on the other hand, people sometimes recover from serious illness without having prayed. Any generalization to the effect that requests of this kind are reliably answered, in the way Elijah's requests are reported to be answered, is demonstrably false.

It would be desirable to develop an account of miracles which would allow us to attribute such events to divine agency without having to predict who will be healed and who will not.

Even if we do not wish to say that miracles still occur, an account of miracles ought to be capable of applying, in principle, to a case like this. And regardless of the possibility of a miracle occurring, modern theists do commonly want to say that God is active in their lives. Someone might, for example, be presented with an unexpected opportunity; she does not claim it is a miracle, but she does say that God's hand was in it. Such a claim should not burden her with the responsibility of being able to predict what God will do in the future.

Against this view, however, one might protest that references to divine agency *always* have some explanatory value when they are capable of making an event intelligible to us, by subsuming it to a theistic worldview; such intelligibility does not depend on our being able to make predictions. Consider the case of the resurrection. Christians want to say that this is to be attributed to divine agency.[12] Certainly Christian theology is prepared to elucidate God's purpose in raising Jesus, and has much to say about the *meaning* of this particular expression of divine agency for the human condition. One might, for example, say that the resurrection was what made reconciliation possible between God and humanity. A fuller explanation of what this means would attempt to make clear the nature of humanity's alienation from God and the importance of this reconciliation for human life and fulfillment. And of course in saying all this, we do not commit ourselves, at least in any obvious way,[13] to the possibility of making any predictions about what God will do in the future. We would be hard-pressed to deny that theology is capable of explaining the religious significance of the resurrection; surely this is one way in which we may make such an event intelligible, in the absence of anything that the natural sciences would admit as an explanation.

If we are concerned about avoiding any confusion with the method of the natural sciences, we might say that we are simply *elucidating* the religious significance of the resurrection, in preference to saying that we are offering an explanation for it. Yet it does not conflict with our ordinary use of the term 'explanation' to say that it is an explanation of the religious significance of the event that we undertake. The important point is that, in explaining it, we are not showing its place in some system of empirical regularities, as the natural sciences would do. We are showing its place within a religious view of the world.

The consequence of this is that the sort of intelligibility that we bring to our experience, when we assimilate it to a religious practice, is quite different from the kind of intelligibility offered to us by the natural sciences. The supernaturalist might now be moved to conclude that here, after all, we have found a way in which the natural sciences may be counted as incomplete, and one in which we must rely on the principles of theistic religion to fill in the story. I have no objection to this. The problem is in saying how it is that filling in the gaps requires any appeal to the supernatural. Admitting that science cannot tell us what significance an event may have for human life seems very far from admitting that supernatural forces are intruding into the natural order. The territory that theology occupies here is not disputed.

Our conclusion, I think, should be that theology can supplement the picture of the world that is given to us by the natural sciences. This is not done, however, by theology's imitating the method of the sciences.

In this chapter we have considered the question of whether it is possible to give an explanation for the occurrence of a miracle that is distinctively supernatural. Nowell-Smith has argued that any adequate explanation must be capable of predictive expansion, but that any explanation that satisfies this requirement will be consistent with the method of the natural sciences, and so cannot serve a supernaturalistic program, which is to say of an event such as a miracle that this is something that could not occur were it not for the existence of entities or powers that are distinctly supernatural. We have considered Paul Dietl's objection to this line of argument; Dietl offers an example of a miracle which may be explained by reference to divine agency, and which is capable of predictive expansion, but which does not fall under the method of the natural sciences.

I have argued that Dietl is wrong about this last claim; there seems to be no reason why the kind of explanation he offers cannot be viewed as falling under the methods of the natural sciences. I have also argued that many of the miracles reported in the Bible – as well as miracles that have been thought to occur since then – cannot be explained in the way Dietl suggests. Yet these can be given robust explanations in terms of their religious significance – showing how they fit into a theistic religious practice. This latter possibility is, I think, intriguing. For if we make a miracle intelligible by articulating its role in a religious practice, the kind of intelligibility we bring to it really does seem to be distinctively religious.

This concludes my criticism of the supernaturalist conception of the miraculous – that is, with the conception of a miracle as *caused by* some supernatural force or entity, where the notion of such a cause closely parallels that of a natural cause. I hope that I have shown that there are enough difficulties with the attempt to conceive miracles in this way to motivate an alternative conception. I turn now to my defense of a teleological conception of the miraculous – one which can operate without identifying God as the *cause* of a miracle. In what follows I will attempt to show that we can conceive of a miracle as expressing divine agency without drawing on any of the presuppositions of supernaturalism.

Chapter 4

Miracle as Basic Action

I have tried to illustrate the problems that come with a supernaturalist picture of miracles. The supernaturalist thinks of a miracle as the intrusion of some supernatural force into the natural world. Drawing on this conception, she points to the occurrence of a miracle as evidence that the natural world is only part of the totality of all that there is, and that we must acknowledge the existence of supernatural powers in addition to the forces of nature. We began our examination of the supernaturalistic conception of the miraculous by looking closely at the notion of a violation of natural law; we noticed that there is no incoherence in the idea of an anomaly – an event that is not determined to occur by physical circumstances. However, we observed that there are no empirical grounds for determining whether an event falls into this category. We have also seen that there is no reason to think of such an event as 'cutting against the grain' of nature, or in any way as disrupting the natural order. In any case the occurrence of such an event is consistent with the tenets of naturalism and so cannot do the work that the supernaturalist would like it to do.

We then considered the possibility that a miracle might be *supernaturally caused*. We noticed a problem for supernaturalism, which is that if the notion of a supernatural cause is drawn too closely to that of a natural cause, it will be hard to say what is really *supernatural* about it; on the other hand, if there is no basis for any analogy between natural and supernatural causes, there will be no grounds for thinking of any supernatural activity as a form of causation. Furthermore, if the supernatural domain is conceived as being radically different from that of nature, we will have trouble saying how it is that there can be any causal interaction between these two domains.

Finally, we examined the claim that an event that fails to have a natural explanation might have one that is supernatural. We discovered that miracles, as conceived within the context of theistic religious practice, seem to fall into two categories. Sometimes a prophet such as Elijah or Moses is represented as being able to work miracles in a regular and predictable manner. Such incidents seem to be susceptible to explanations that are empirically testable, yet for this very reason, they fail to point to the existence of anything beyond the realm of nature; that is, they are entirely consistent with naturalism. I have argued, however, that the requirement that all explanations be testable in this way is too stringent. It seems as though, faced with an anomaly of some kind, we can attribute its occurrence to divine agency, and that doing this serves to make the event intelligible to us; that is, it has explanatory value. However, this does not seem to be involved with the possibility of making predictions. On the contrary, it seems to arise from the fact that in attributing something to divine agency, we make it possible to assimilate it to a theistic religious practice. The sort of explanation we offer in this case is, of course, quite different from the sort by which the natural sciences operate. Nevertheless, there does not seem to be anything particularly *supernatural* about such explanations. Our assimilation of such an event to a religious practice does not require us to admit that any supernatural force is intruding into the natural world.

What we have accomplished up to this point is largely negative; I have given reasons for rejecting a supernaturalist account of miracles. I wish now to begin developing a positive account of the miraculous. Using the categories that I developed in my Introduction, my own account may be described as non-supernaturalistic; I want to argue that events might occur that would be consistent with the naturalistic worldview, yet nevertheless qualify as miracles. To put the point differently: we have seen the difficulty involved in saying what sort of event might be inconsistent with the tenets of naturalism; fortunately this difficulty does not stand in the way of our being able to describe what sort of event would, if it occurred, qualify as a miracle.

The account of miracles I wish to develop in this chapter is a teleological one; that is, I wish to develop a notion of 'miracle' by which a miracle is to be understood as an action on the part of God. I also hope to argue, in my final chapter, for a *contextual* conception of 'miracle', according to which an event is to be understood as miraculous by virtue of the circumstances in which it occurs.

I will give only a brief argument in favor of our adopting a teleological conception of miracles. My primary purpose in the present chapter will be to show how such an account may avoid the problems that beset supernaturalism. I am particularly interested to defend two related theses, namely (a) that we may defend a teleological conception of the miraculous without committing ourselves to saying that God is the supernatural *cause* of a miracle, and (b) that we do not have to eliminate the possibility that an event has a natural cause in order to qualify as an expression of divine agency, and as a miracle. Some miracles might turn out to be genuine anomalies; others might have natural explanations. I will argue that it does not matter which of these we take to be the case. We may embrace a position of 'nomic agnosticism' when it comes to miracles – that is, we need not determine whether or not an event conforms to the laws of nature in order to describe it as a miracle. The point is simply that the conception of a miracle has no proper reference to natural law.

My account will depend heavily on the analogy between divine and human action. I will begin by calling attention to the fact that we may identify cases in which a human agent may act in doing *x* without its being the case that she *causes x* to occur. This is true when *x* is a *basic action*. Furthermore, basic actions are instances of human agency even though they may be described as having natural causes. I hope to show how we may say the same of a divine action, where this is conceived as *basic* divine agency.

In the previous chapters we have seen that quite often, the supernaturalist account seems to offer an account of supernatural causation that is muddled; confusing teleological questions – 'Is this event something *done by* God?' – with causal ones – 'Does this event have a supernatural cause?' My main concern in this chapter is with disentangling these issues.

Before closing this chapter I want to consider an objection to the analogy between the basic actions of human beings and God, which is that the basic actions of humans are generally identified with bodily movements, whereas God is not normally conceived as possessing a body. I will briefly examine, without defending, the suggestion that the physical universe is itself the body of God; I will then adduce two counter-examples to the claim that basic actions must always be expressed in bodily movements, first pointing to the occurrence of basic *mental* events, and then to the conceptual possibility that basic agency could be imputed to someone possessing telekinetic powers.

Must 'Miracle' Be Conceived Teleologically?

I propose to give a teleological account of the miraculous. Not everyone is agreed that miracles must be understood teleologically; therefore, I will say something to defend the claim that we need such an account.

First, it seems to me that a non-teleological account must rely heavily on supernaturalistic assumptions. Thus, for example, one might wish to say that it is sufficient for an event's being a miracle that it be a violation of natural law, or that it have a supernatural cause.[1] To the extent that I have been successful in undermining the supernaturalist conception of the miraculous, I have given reasons for rejecting what is, as far as I can determine, the principal alternative to a teleological account. If supernaturalism fails to give us a workable account of the miraculous, then a teleological account seems to be all we have left.

As an additional consideration, I would suggest that the philosophically interesting applications[2] of the term occur primarily within the context of theistic religion, where miracles are generally seen as expressing divine agency. Now it is true that miracle stories occur within the context of non-theistic religious traditions; as an example one might consider the reports of miraculous events surrounding the birth of the Buddha.[3] One might argue that these events may be conceived teleologically without being understood in theistic terms, but I cannot explore this issue here. My present concern is with how the notion of a miracle works in a theistic religion like Christianity.

One might stipulate a special sense of 'miracle' by which any event failing to be subsumable under natural law qualifies as miraculous, even in the absence of its having any role to play in the plans of some deity. I have no objection to such a stipulation. However, I cannot see any utility in it. If such events are not thought of as having any connection to divine agency, it is hard to see what part they might play within theistic religion; it is even more difficult to see what other area of human inquiry might hold a place for them. Certainly they have no role to play in the natural sciences.

Divine Agency Without Supernatural Causation

In the previous chapters we saw the difficulty that comes with a supernaturalist account of the miraculous, and I am hoping now to construct a non-causal account of miracles. Thus the question we now face is: How can we say that a miracle expresses divine agency without this implying that God supernaturally *caused* it to occur? Judging from the literature on miracles, it seems to be quite natural to assume that divine agency is synonymous with divine causation – that to say 'God did *x*' is to say that God *caused x* to occur. It is generally assumed that if God caused *x* to occur then *x* has a supernatural cause. Of course *x* would have a supernatural cause in this case – so it might be argued; God is the cause of *x* and God is a supernatural entity.

As we have seen, however, this leaves the believer in miracles in a bit of a quandary. For it is difficult to say how it is that a supernatural entity can have any causal influence over natural events. In order to defend the suggestion that God is the cause of an event in nature, we must show how an interaction is possible between the natural and the supernatural domains. And as we saw in Chapter 3, the claim that such interactions take place is untenable.

The solution to our problem comes when we recognize that it is not the case that all actions are *caused* by their agents to occur. Those who insist on a causal analysis of miracles overlook the possibility that a miracle is a *basic action* on God's part.

The term 'basic act' is due to Arthur Danto, although Wittgenstein seems to have been aware of the need to include basic actions in our talk of human agency (1968: I, 614), as was A. I. Melden (1961). The nineteenth-century American theologian Horace Bushnell (1860: 44) also shows an understanding of their character in his own account of miracles.[4] Danto defines a basic action as one which its agent does not cause to occur (1965: 142; 1968: 42). When he claims that some of my actions are basic, what he wants to say is that some of my actions are such that I perform them immediately or directly, without doing anything else first:

> When an individual *M* performs a basic action *a*, there is no event distinct from *a* that both stands to *a* as cause to effect *and* is an action performed by *M*. So when *M* performs a basic action, he does nothing first that causes it to happen. (1968: 43)

Danto's account of the difference between basic and non-basic actions was the subject of considerable criticism. Many philosophers have offered refinements to this notion, among them Alvin Goldman (1976), Jennifer Hornsby (1980), and Donald Davidson (1982). I will not explore this discussion in detail. However, two problems stand out. First, suppose that Sally turns on a light by flipping a switch, and that she flips the switch by moving her fingers in a certain way. No doubt what Danto wants to say is that Sally moved her fingers as a basic action, because there is nothing else that Sally had to do in order to move them. By contrast, in order to turn on the light, Sally had to move her fingers, thereby flipping the switch; her turning on the light ought to be a basic action. But Danto's analysis does not have this result. Consider Sally's act in turning on the light – that is, consider the act that is singled out by the description 'Sally's turning on of the light'. Given Danto's definition, Sally's turning on of the light will be a non-basic action if there is no other act that Sally must do to bring it about. But Sally does not do anything else to bring it about that she turns on the light; that is, Sally does not cause herself to turn on the light. Thus Sally's turning on the light turns out, on Danto's analysis, to be a basic action.[5] Surely this is not what Danto intended to say.

Danto also seems to have overlooked the fact that there are more varieties of basicness than just *causal* basicness. For example I may dance the waltz by moving my left foot forward, then moving my right foot to the side, and so on. Moving my left foot forward seems to be a basic action; at least, it is more basic than my waltzing. However, the relationship between my various foot movements and my waltzing does not seem to be a causal one. This is an example of an action that might be referred to as *compositionally* more basic than my doing the waltz (Hornsby 1980: 68). Alternatively, I may signal for a turn by putting my arm out of the window. But the relationship between my putting my arm out the window, and my signaling for a turn, is not a causal one. It seems, rather, to be one of convention; it is convention that determines that I signal for a turn by putting my arm out of the window (Goldman 1976: 25).

Despite the fact that causal basicness is only one sort of basicness, it is primarily causal basicness that concerns us here, and I want to pursue this notion by considering how Donald Davidson describes the phenomenon. Davidson does not use the term 'basic', but prefers to speak of *primitive actions*:

> Not every event we attribute to an agent can be explained as caused by another event of which he is agent: some acts must be primitive in the sense that they cannot be analysed in terms of their causal relations to acts of the same agent. But then event causality cannot in this way be used to explain the relation between an agent and a primitive action. Event causality can spread responsibility for an action to the consequences of the action, but it cannot help explicate the first attribution of agency on which the rest depend. (1982: 49)

In order to see what Davidson has in mind here, let us consider his example (1982: 53). Suppose I intentionally move my fingers, thereby flicking a switch, which causes a light to come on, which illuminates a room, which alerts a prowler.[6] The prowler's being alerted is connected to my agency by a chain of causes. The cause of the prowler's being alerted is the room's being illuminated; the cause of the room's being illuminated is the light's coming on; the cause of the light's coming on is the switch's being flicked. What Davidson wants to say is that we cannot give a complete analysis of my action in terms of this kind of event causation – that such a causal analysis must culminate in an action that is primitive (or basic) – in this case, my moving of my fingers. This primary, primitive, or basic action of mine has, as we see, a good number of consequences, and all of these consequences may be attributed to my agency by virtue of being consequences of my primitive or basic act. Thus, for example, there is a chain of causes connecting the movement of my fingers with the light's turning on; for this reason, I may be said to have acted in turning on the light. As Davidson says, once I move my fingers, 'each consequence presents us with a deed; an agent causes what his actions cause' (1982: 53).

Thus we may say that I alert the prowler by illuminating the room, that I illuminate the room by turning on the light, that I turn on the light by flicking the switch, and that I flick the switch by moving my fingers. But I do not move my fingers by doing anything else; I just move them. A basic action, then, is one that I do not perform by doing anything else. A basic, or primitive, action is one that its agent 'just does'.

Associating my agency with, for example, the light's turning on requires a causal analysis; we must have reason to say that I am the cause of this event. But it is important to see that it is not the case for every event in the chain. The causal series has to have a starting point in something that I 'just do', without my having to do anything else. If we suppose that everything I do, I do by doing something else, then we are caught in an infinite regress; in order to move my fingers I would have to do something else (x), and in order to do x I would have to do something else (y), and in order to do y I would have to do z, and so on *ad infinitum*. Thus if we were to say that every event that may be associated with my agency is one that I cause to occur, I could never really *start* acting.

It seems to me that a further observation is possible, which is that I do not *cause* my fingers to move. There could be controversy about this. All we have really established, at most, is that my agency is not attributed to my basic actions by means of an *event-causal* analysis; there is nothing that I do, other than simply moving my fingers, to cause them to move. I do think that, in general, when we speak of causes it is *event* causation that we are talking about. Still, a critic may wish to argue that there is some other sort of cause that might be operating in the case of my basic actions. If this kind of cause is to be associated with my *doing* something, then the most likely way of making this out would be to invoke a sense of causation that is inherently teleological or intentional. I will grant for the sake of argument that such an account may be correct. It will be sufficient for my purposes that the notion of causation is not that of event causation, and that references to this special sort of causation will be, in principle, teleological. It is, after all, my goal here to argue for a teleological conception of 'miracle'; if this is made out in terms of a particularly teleological conception of causation, I see no reason why it should not be compatible with the picture of miracles that I wish to give.

Thus in proposing to give a non-causal account of miracles, I do not intend to offer reasons for ruling out the idea that there might be some conception of causation that might have a role to play in our analysis of basic actions. My commitment is to the claim that, if we conceive miracles as basic actions on the part of God, we do not have to think of God as bringing them about in an event-causal sort of way.

Now it seems quite clear that, if God is to act at all, then God must perform basic actions; if we deny this, then as we have seen, we entangle ourselves in an infinite regress. Not even an omnipotent being could act, if that being could not *commence* acting in the performance of a basic action. Some philosophers have been skeptical of accounts of divine agency that appeal to the notion of a basic action; for example, Nicholas Saunders has referred, in what I take to be a disparaging way, to the assertion that 'God is active in some unexplained direct sense without the need for mediating causal interactions' (2002: 39ff.). But if we are to suppose that God acts at all, then we *must* suppose that every act that God performs will either be a basic action, or will be associated with an event that traces its causal ancestry to something that God does as a basic action. We cannot avoid facing up to the fact that God is active in just the sort of unexplained – and *unexplainable* – direct sense that

Saunders seems to find so troublesome. It seems to me that the only real point of controversy, then, will be over *which* events are to be associated with divine agency in this direct sense, and which may be properly said to be caused by God.

I am interested in some very significant implications of the view that a miracle is – or may be associated with – a basic divine action. First, it eliminates the interaction problem. To speak of God as the agent of a miracle does not require us to defend the possibility of a causal interaction between nature and the supernatural. Second, it provides us with a way to associate divine agency with events that are anomalous or uncaused. And finally, it allows us a way to associate divine agency with events that have natural causes.

Miracles and Interaction

Perhaps the most obvious benefit in speaking of miracles as basic divine actions is that it relieves us from the need to articulate how it is that God can exert a causal influence over events in nature from the other side of a supposed natural/supernatural divide. As we saw in Chapter 2, the idea that causal interactions take place between the two different domains of nature and supernature brings with it difficulties similar to those encountered by the sub-stance dualist, who insists that mind or spirit can effect bodily changes. We really have no conception of how such an interaction might be possible. But the interaction problem arises from our attempt to think of God as the cause of a miracle. We are relieved of the difficulties that come with trying to explain how a causal interaction can span a divide between two domains if we do not accept any requirement to think of God's activity in the natural world in causal terms.

To put the matter somewhat differently: we may be perplexed as to how God, conceived as a transcendent being, can act in the natural world. Suppose, for example, we want to say that God has turned water into wine. But we may be perplexed as to how God can turn water into wine. Part of our perplexity has nothing to do with God; we simply do not know how it is that water can turn into wine. This is because we have no idea what sort of *natural* process would account for the transformation of water into wine, i.e. we do not see what sort of *natural* cause might be responsible for such a thing.

The second dimension of our perplexity has to do with the question of how *God* can turn water into wine, that is, what means God can employ in doing this. We have no idea what sort of natural means God might employ, since as we just noted, we have no idea what sort of natural process might account for water's turning into wine. Now if we take the usual supernaturalistic approach we will say that God is not limited to the employment of a natural means in bringing it about that water turns into wine. There is more than just nature, after all, and there are more causes than just natural ones. God may employ a *supernatural* means in turning the water into wine. But we are in no better shape now than we were when we tried to imagine what sort of natural process might result in water's turning to wine. For we have no better conception of how any supposed *supernatural* process could have this result, either – particularly since we have no idea how a causal interaction might span the boundary that supernaturalism supposes to exist between the domains of nature and the supernatural.[7]

If there are only two varieties of causal means that God might employ in turning water into wine, and we cannot conceive of how God might make use of either one, then it seems we have only two options left to us. We can say that God cannot turn water into wine. But this is to turn our back on miracles – and also, one would think, to turn our backs on divine omnipotence. Alternatively, we can say that God *employs no means* in turning water into wine – that God's turning of water into wine is a basic action on God's part. Given the difficulties that attend our speaking of God as causing water to turn into wine, where this implies that God employs some means in doing this, I advocate that we think of this as a divine basic action. And it is important to see that this is compatible with the view that the event, to be described as water's turning into wine, is an anomaly – an event that, being undetermined, has no cause at all. Saying that the water's turning into wine has no cause is entirely compatible with saying that God turned the water into wine, where this refers to an action on the part of God.

Miracles and Natural Causes

I have argued that if we conceive of miracles as divine basic actions, we eliminate the interaction problem, i.e. we are relieved of the difficulties that attend our speaking of God as acting causally across a natural/supernatural divide. We have also noted that there is nothing stopping us from associating an anomaly with divine agency. I wish now to show that conceiving of miracles as divine basic actions relieves us of the obligation to show that a purported miracle has no natural cause. A key component of my argument will be to draw on an analogy to human agency. When I raise my arm in a basic way, it is possible to say that I am acting, without having to eliminate the possibility that the event we may describe as my arm's rising has a physical cause. Quite to the contrary, we would most likely *assume* that this event has a natural cause, no doubt to be made out in terms of muscular contractions and neural firings. I want to suggest that the same is true of divine agency.

Suppose I raise my arm, and that I do this as a basic action. We may say that my action in raising my arm involves, or is associated with, a particular event, namely my arm's rising. Indeed it seems as though the fact that I have acted in raising my arm implies that an event has occurred, which may be described as my arm's rising; I have no idea how it would be possible for me to raise my arm even though my arm did not rise, e.g. it remained located at my side. (Notice that the converse is not true; my arm might rise, perhaps as the result of a spasm, without my having raised it.) Let us say that a basic action may generally be associated with a *companion event*; in this case, the companion event with respect to my act of raising my arm would be my arm's rising. What I want to say is that the possibility that I have acted, in raising my arm, is not diminished by the fact that the companion event that accompanies my action, namely my arm's rising, has a natural explanation which may be filled out in event-causal terms, by reference to neural firings and so on.[8]

Let us now consider how this might work in the case of a miracle. Consider the case of God's action in turning water into wine. This action is associated with a companion event, which we may describe as the water's turning into wine. Suppose now that physicists are able to describe a natural process by which water may turn into wine; perhaps this will have something to do with the behavior of subatomic particles. The possibility that God has acted, in turning the water into wine, is not diminished by the fact that the companion event that accompanies God's action, namely the water's turning into wine, has a natural explanation.

I would like to highlight a particular advantage that such an account brings, which is that it renders our references to divine agency immune from the charge of redundancy by appeal to the principle of Ockham's Razor. It is commonly thought that if a natural explanation is discovered for a putative miracle, this will mean that any reference to divine agency will be otiose. The conventional wisdom is that this would imply an overdetermination for the event in question. However, the event will be overdetermined only if we are trying to supply two independently sufficient event-causal explanations for it. When we attribute the event to God's basic agency, we are not attempting to account for its occurrence in event-causal terms. No one would say that an explanation for my arm's rising, in terms of neural firings and the like, renders otiose an agentive account by which I am understood as intentionally raising my hand – to hail a taxi, for example, or to bid at auction. Thus giving a natural explanation for a putative miracle will not make it redundant to attribute it to God's agency, as long as it is God's *basic* agency of which we speak.

Miracle, Mystery, and the God-of-the-gaps

In giving an account of the conception of a miracle, it is important to recognize that a miracle is an inherently *mysterious* event. As we have already noticed, it is one of the most fundamental components of the concept of 'miracle' that a miracle is a *wonder*. Indeed part of the criticism that might be made of the supernaturalistic conception of a miracle is that it does not preserve this element. This is due to the tendency of the supernaturalistically minded apologist to model her account of the miraculous on a scientific analysis. Of course such an apologist does not wish to say that a miracle can be explained by science – it is very important for her to deny this, in order to give grounds for her competing explanation. The apologist wants to point to the scientific account as leaving gaps in our understanding of the world, and she proposes to fill in these gaps with a theological account. But in order to compete with the scientific worldview in this way, theology must be reconstructed as an analog to science, appealing to its own kind of forces and its own distinctive form of causation. Given the occurrence of a miracle, such as the resurrection of Jesus, the apologist wants to argue that science cannot explain how this could have happened; theology must step up to fill in the gaps. This strategy is reminiscent of what D. Z. Phillips has referred to as 'open-door epistemology':

> The advocate of open-door epistemology appeals to miracles as though they were alternative ways of getting things done; ways which show that science does not have a monopoly in these matters. The trouble is that his suggestion remains within the grammar of a science-like discourse. It is not content to remain with the inexplicable character of miracles. On this view, there must be an explanation of inexplicable events. It is said that we human beings do not know what the explanation is. But, of course, so the argument runs, God does. Thus God is turned into a super-scientist. Such religious advocacy shares a common assumption with scientism: there must be an explanation for everything. God, or the miracle worker, on this view, simply makes use of knowledge (the way of bringing things about we call miracles) which is unavailable to the vast majority of mankind. (1999: 135)

Theistic religion, however, is not prepared to explain how Jesus might come back alive after being dead for three days. We might suppose that God has some secret technique by which he was able to do this – that he employed some means in bringing it about. But of course this would be to assume that the resurrection was a non-basic action on God's part, and were we to insist on such a picture of things, our insistence would give every appearance of being motivated by the assumption that for everything that is done, there is a *means* by which it is done. Yet we have seen that this is not true. An agent employs no means in bringing about her basic actions. Thus if we treat the resurrection as a basic action on the part of God, we are relieved of any obligation to find a means by which God raised Jesus from the dead.[9] I would suggest that this counts in favor of our treating this as a basic action, and against our speculating about the existence of a mechanism for the resurrection.

If we treat a miracle, such as the resurrection, as a basic action on God's part, this relieves us of the need to speak of how God brought it about. Indeed we might say that it makes clear why the possibility of giving such an account is ruled out. In asking how God performs a miracle, we presume that God employed a means in doing so. But if the resurrection is a basic divine action, then God employed no means in bringing it about that Jesus returned to life. Nature, we may say, immediately expresses the will of God in the same way in which my arm immediately expresses my will to raise it. In this case, too, the mystery remains. I do not explain *how* I raise my arm when I identify this as a basic action of mine; indeed I make it clear that there is no 'how' of it. If the resurrection is a divine basic action, such 'how' questions are similarly out of place. Thus the force of our identifying the resurrection as a divine basic action is to treat the mystery of its occurrence as irremediable. Theistic religion does not attempt to fill in the gaps here, but acknowledges them.

Chapter 5

Miracle and Divine Agency

After considering the difficulties that attend a supernaturalistic conception of 'miracle', I have begun a reconstruction of this notion that hopes to avoid these difficulties by finding an alternative to speaking of a miracle as supernaturally caused. An important step in my proposal is to conceive miracles as basic actions on the part of God. A basic action is one that its agent 'just does', and does not do by doing anything else. That is, in thinking of an agent as performing a basic action, we do not think of her as employing any means to do what she does. If miracles are basic divine actions, then there is no need to speak of how God causes them to come about; indeed the search for such a cause is motivated by a confusion about the character of God's agency – it rests upon the false assumption that everything an agent does is something that she causes to occur.

I have also tried to show that, if we conceive a miracle to be a basic action on the part of God, we do not have to show that it has no natural cause. A divine action may supervene on an event or process that is naturally explicable. Thus being able to speak of miracles as basic divine actions solves a good number of very thorny problems. We do not have to speak of God as the supernatural cause of a miracle, nor defend an interactionist metaphysics by explaining how a supernatural entity such as God can interact causally with objects in nature. Perhaps most importantly, we do not have to achieve the seemingly impossible task of showing that an event has no natural cause before attributing it to divine agency.

I want to devote this chapter to some problems that may be seen to attend an account of miracles as basic divine actions. My particular focus will be on the notion of basic divine agency in its own right, without regard to the particular question of how such agency might express itself in a miracle. The first problem is that, if we speak of God as engaging in basic actions, we may be committed to saying that the world is God's body. Yet there seem to be significant disanalogies between the relationship that a human being has to her body, and the relationship that God has to the world. I will be concerned here to argue that an account of miracles as basic divine actions is not committed to viewing the world as God's body.

A second objection to the suggestion that God acts in the world in a basic way is that it fails to acknowledge a need to give an account of the causal means by which God acts in the world. This objection is generally connected with the search for the 'causal joint' by which God's will may be understood as connecting to, or interfacing with, natural processes. Some philosophers have been concerned to locate divine agency in 'gappy' or undetermined phenomena of some kind, such as those represented by the states of subatomic particles. In giving a response to this line of thought I will try to bring out some of the implications of an account of basic divine agency for the problem of the causal joint – most importantly, that the joint between divine agency and natural processes, such as it is, is not a causal one. I will also argue that, absent special considerations to the contrary that may arise in a particular case, we ought to locate basic divine agency at the level of ordinary experience, rather than at the level of microprocesses such as quantum events. I will be concerned to show how this may be done.

I begin with a discussion of basic actions and the prospect of our thinking of the world as God's body.

The World as God's Body

An objection that might be made to the conception of miracles as basic actions is that basic actions in humans typically express themselves in bodily movements. We might imagine a critic charging that this is an important part of the concept of a basic action – that any being lacking a body cannot be said to engage in basic actions. And of course since God is not customarily thought of as having a body, we would thus lack an important part of the basis for attributing basic actions to God.

One response to this objection would be to suppose that the physical universe itself is the body of God. This is a view that can be found in Indian theism, particularly in the work of Ramanuja, a thirteenth-century philosopher writing in the Vaishnava tradition. Related conceptions were not unusual in ancient Western philosophy – Plato suggested in the *Timaeus* that the world had a soul, and the Stoic conception of the *logos* seems roughly similar.

In contemporary philosophy, Grace Jantzen (1984) develops a similar view, which she takes to be a natural implication of the suggestion that God's actions in the world are basic. Charles Hartshorne also argues that we ought to understand the world as God's body. He considers two principal analogies that have been used in the history of theology to understand the relation of human beings to God; the first is what he calls the 'interpersonal' metaphor, which was adopted by Judaic theology, according to which the relation of human beings to God is thought of as similar to the relation between a child and her parent. In contrast, the Greek conception (via Plato) – which Hartshorne prefers – was that of 'the relation of a person or soul as conscious individual to the physical body of that individual' (1983: 54). On this view God becomes the 'World Soul', and Hartshorne explicitly invokes the analogy between God-World and Soul-Body (1983: 61).

Richard Swinburne also comments on this issue. He, too, has noticed (1979: 48) that some, at least, of the actions of God would be basic actions, such as 'keeping the universe in existence and keeping the behaviour of things in conformity with natural laws'; the creation of matter *ex nihilo* and changing the characteristics of existing things are other examples. This latter sort of exercise would appear to cover miracles, and so it seems likely that Swinburne would endorse the proposition that miracles are, by and large, to be understood as basic actions. He addresses the question of God's embodiment in the world, noticing that embodiment generally has four features: someone who is embodied (1) can move parts of their body as basic actions; (2) is (immediately) aware of what is happening in or to their body, and is aware of what happens outside their body (and gains knowledge of it) only by virtue of the effects of the outside world on their body, such as light rays impinging on their eyes; (3) an embodied being looks out on the world from where their body is, and (4) the thoughts and feelings of an embodied being are affected by disturbances in the body – 'disturbances in the table or the body over there are not felt by me' (1979: 49). Swinburne asserts that 'a person has a body if there is a material object to which he is related in all of the above four ways', and that 'clearly a person does not have a body if there is no material object to which he is related in any of the above ways' (ibid.). The odd case arises when there is a being that is related to a material object in some, but not all, of these ways – and God falls into this category. Of these criteria God satisfies only the first, on Swinburne's view, i.e. God is embodied, but only to a degree, that is, only in respect of God's ability to move physical objects in a basic way.

More recently, Sally McFague has defended the view that the universe is God's body; such a view provides a basis for what she refers to as an 'ecological theology' (1993).

On the other hand, the suggestion that the world is the body of God has been criticized by John Polkinghorne, who notices some important disanalogies between the relation of God to the universe, and the relation of human beings to their bodies. For one thing, there does not seem to be anything in the universe answering to the nervous system in human beings; the exercise of human agency depends on a properly functioning nervous system. Another problem is that 'in our psychosomatic nature we are constituted by our bodies, and in consequence we are in thrall to them as they change, eventually dying with their decay' (2003: 57).

I would prefer to remain neutral on the issue of whether the universe ought to be considered God's body. Clearly, if God acts in a basic way in the natural world, there is basis for comparison to the relation that human beings have to their bodies; as Polkinghorne points out, however, this comparison has its limitations. For now I will argue that an agent's basic actions need not be expressed in bodily movements – and I will do this through the use of two counter-examples. One is real, and the other is, as far as I know, imaginary.

Basic Mental Acts

We are considering, as an objection to our account of miracles as basic divine actions, the fact that there is what appears to be a significant disanalogy between the basic acts of human beings, and miracles as the basic acts of God, and that is that the basic acts of human beings are generally – or perhaps, most obviously – expressed in bodily movements. But we should not suppose that all of the basic acts of human beings are like this. A basic action need not be realized in a bodily movement. For one thing, *mental* acts may be basic as well. Danto points out (1968: 57) that the distinction between basic and mediated acts can be made in the mental world; there may be some mental acts which I am able to perform only by first performing other acts, such as my first silently reciting a mnemonic poem in order to recall the value of pi to the tenth decimal place. However, there are some mental acts – probably the majority of the mental acts that any of us performs – that are not like this. If I think of a flower, I do not have to do anything else in order to think of it; I may just *think* of it.

It is interesting to think of God as having the same sort of direct control over nature that we have over our own imaginations. To carry out this analogy fully would seem to require embracing some form of panpsychism. I cannot, however, give this possibility adequate attention here. Let it suffice for us to notice that we are not *required* to embrace any form of mentalistic metaphysics in order to say that God may act, in a basic sort of way, in nature. The point here, in any case, is that, if we may be said to act mentally, and if mental acts may be basic, then it is not a conceptual requirement for the performance of a basic action that it be expressed in a bodily movement.

Psychokinesis as Basic Act

A second instance of a non-bodily basic action would be psychokinesis. Now as far as I know, psychokinetic actions do not take place. However, it is at least *conceptually* possible that they might, and if so, this shows that there is nothing in the conception of a basic action that forbids its extension to psychokinesis. Indeed let us suppose that Wilma is able to move objects merely by an effort of her will – i.e. when she wills that a fork bend, the fork bends. In this case the bending of the fork is, as we might say, a direct or immediate expression of Wilma's intention that it bend, in much the same way that my movement of my own arm is a direct or immediate expression of my intention that *it* move. Now everyone wants to know how Wilma can bend forks in this way; what does she do in order to make the fork bend? She can no more tell us how she does this than she can tell us what she does in order to move her arms and legs, because of course there *is* nothing she does in order to bring any of these things about.

Terence Penelhum defends the possibility of accounting for psychokinetic activity on the part of disembodied spirits by speaking of this in terms of basic agency. However, he wants to say that if a spirit were to raise a table as a basic action, then 'the table, at least at the time when it is raised, becomes temporarily the body of the spirit' (1970: 42). His reasoning is that if there is nothing that the spirit has to do in order to raise the table, 'then the analogy with the physical movements of the embodied person's body is as close as it can be, and why not draw the conclusion?' (ibid.). I think, however, that in light of Polkinghorne's observations that we considered above, the analogy is not as close as can be after all. I am more inclined to agree with Vernon White, who suggests we think of 'God's impinging on the animate and inanimate world as a kind of telekinetic basic action – *not* implying any bodily mediation', as Vernon White describes this possibility (1985: 104, emphasis mine). Indeed if human agents were capable of psychokinesis, there would be obvious utility in distinguishing what they do in terms of bodily movements, and what they do *without* the need to move their bodies; it seems difficult to see what other means we could employ to distinguish telekinetic from non-telekinetic acts. Even in the case of disembodied spirits, the most useful way of describing their telekinetic powers is to say that they are able to do what they do *without* the benefit of a body.

Richard Swinburne discusses the possibility of giving a personal explanation in terms of an agent's telekinetic ability:

When presented with a purported demonstration of telekinesis, we may accept a man's having the intention to bend a fork and his power to do so as explaining why a fork at some distance from himself is bent, without our having any idea what his power depended on, and indeed even if we deny that it depends on something. Of course we may reject this explanation, but the point is that it is a logically possible explanation and we do not need to have a belief about some physical state or law being necessary for the exercise of the power in order to accept the purported explanation . . . Personal explanations may explain without there being a scientific explanation of the occurrence. (1979: 47ff.)

Let us set aside for now the question of whether we can *explain* the bending of the fork in the manner described by Swinburne. What is interesting for our purposes at the moment is that, as Swinburne notices, we may attribute the bending of the forks to Wilma's agency without being able to say anything about how she does it. Indeed it is the fact that she does not appear to be employing any means in bending the forks that requires us to view this as an instance of basic agency. Swinburne points out the precedent for such judgements in the phenomenon of basic actions, since we have 'given and accepted explanations, in terms of the agent's intentions, of the actions which they have performed, for many millennia without knowing anything about the physical conditions which are necessary for the agent to possess the power in question' (1979: 47). The point here would seem to be this: if we can say that Wilma raises her arm without knowing how she does it, then the fact that we have no idea how she may bend forks at a distance should not stand in our way of calling that a basic action, either.

In response the critic may say that we should refuse to believe that someone can bend forks without employing any means, since our only precedent for any such 'meansless doing' is in bodily actions. But – again, as Swinburne notices (1979: 47) – this is an epistemological issue, and so does not indicate any *conceptual* problem with identifying Wilma's bending of a fork as a basic action. It is not my concern here to say whether we could ever prove a case of psychokinesis, or even what would count as such a proof. It is enough for us to notice that there does not seem to be any conceptual problem with saying that someone might act in a basic way by bending a fork, and this implies that there is no conceptual problem with extending the discourse of basic actions beyond the domain of bodily movements.

In conclusion, then, it seems to me that in saying that God acts in nature in a basic way, we are not committed to defending the claim that the universe is the body of God. I have no strong objection to this claim, though I acknowledge that there are disanalogies between the relation of God to the world and the relation of human beings to their bodies. But an account of a miracle as divine action is not, as far as I can determine, committed in either direction on this issue.

Non-Basic Divine Agency

I turn now to a discussion of the idea that we cannot avoid speaking of the means that God employs in acting in the world. I have been arguing for a teleological conception of 'miracle', which is to say that I have been arguing that we ought to conceive a miracle in exclusively intentional, or teleological, terms. The way to do this is to think of a miracle as a basic action on the part of God, which is to say that God does not, at least typically, employ any means in bringing a miracle about.

I do not, however, want to say that identifying x as a basic divine action will be sufficient for its being miraculous. There may be divine basic actions that are not miracles. Nor do I want to say that God cannot act in a non-basic way. Sometimes it will be appropriate to speak of God as employing a means in doing what God does. It seems perfectly correct to say, for example, that God freed the Israelites from bondage *by* parting the Red Sea; God's liberation of the Israelites would thus be a non-basic action on God's part.

Let us consider another example. Suppose that Sister Gwendolyn buys a lottery ticket, hoping to fund an orphanage if she wins. Her lottery numbers are selected by a process which, by a purely physical analysis, must be counted as random; given the physical forces at work, each lottery ball has an equal likelihood of being selected. Yet when her numbers are chosen, she counts this as an expression of God's grace. Subsequently she may say that God funded the orphanage, speaking of this as a divine action, and she may go on to explain that God funded the orphanage *by* making it the case that the appropriate numbers were selected. God's funding the orphanage would thus be a non-basic action, and under the circumstances I have no objection to the claim that God *caused* the orphanage to be funded, where this implies a means or mechanism that God employed in bringing this about. (Here, of course, the mechanism is a natural one.) On the other hand, it will be possible to think of God's making it the case that this particular set of numbers (*S*) was selected as God's basic action; if we describe things in this way, then we do not think of God as doing anything else in order to insure that these numbers are selected.

Divine Agency and Non-determined Processes

I have acknowledged that there may be cases in which it is appropriate to think of God as employing a means in doing what God does. We are considering a case in which God funds a charity by bringing it about that a nun wins the lottery. I have suggested, however, that in such a case we will still think of God as doing something in a basic way, and I have spoken of this as making it the case that a particular set (*S*) of lottery numbers falls from the machine. I wish now to digress slightly and say something about how God's agency might be associated with a random process, such as the selection of a set of lottery numbers. In doing so I anticipate a discussion that I will give later in this chapter, in regard to the connection that we might make between divine agency and non-determined processes generally.[1]

A critic may not be satisfied with the claim that God acts basically in selecting the set of lottery numbers *S*. He may insist that we press the question and ask *how* God did this. Supposing that the numbers were chosen by tumbling lottery balls in a machine of some kind, the critic may insist that there is some mechanism connecting God's intention that the set of balls *S* be chosen with the fact that *S* was chosen. We normally suppose that the outcome of a lottery drawing is something that occurs by chance, i.e. that numbers are selected randomly. But this was no random outcome. God must have *caused* S to be chosen – giving this ball a nudge to the right, perhaps with a little gust of air, holding this one back just a little bit as the other balls tumble, and so on. Thus on this view the selection of S really is physically determined after all, but this determination results from divine action, a divine manipulation of physical forces sufficient to guarantee the result that God intends. On this view God brings about the selection of S in the same way that a lottery cheat would select them, by manipulating the physical forces operating during the selection process in order to force a particular outcome. The critic's account here would seem to imply that the selection of S was not actually a random process after all.

I think that this response involves a confusion. First, we should notice that the term 'random' may be used as an antonym to 'purpose', as in 'George chose his targets at random', which tells us that George had no reason for selecting any particular target. In this sense of 'random', to deny that S was selected at random is only to insist that S was selected for a reason, that is, that God *acted* in making it the case that S fell from the lottery machine, in order to fund Sister Gwendolyn's orphanage. Denying that the selection of S was random in this sense has teleological implications. Its force is to say that the falling of the lottery balls is implicated in an action – something done for a reason.

But there is another sense of 'random'. In this second sense, when we deny that an event occurs at random, we mean to say that the process by which it occurred was physically predisposed to produce it. To deny that an event occurs at random in this second sense does not carry any teleological implications. It only serves to describe the physical process by which the event came about. This being the case, it seems to be open to us to insist that something has happened for a reason – thereby denying that it is random in the teleological sense – while allowing that it is the result of a process that may be described as random in the second, non-teleological, sense.

In order to see how this is possible, let us begin by noticing that an act description introduces an event description.[2] Thus, for example, a description of Sally as *starting the car* is an act description, and it introduces an event description, namely *the car's starting*. (We have previously referred to the latter as a *companion event*.) Now let us consider the prospect of God's action in making it the case that S, the set of lottery balls that will make Sister Gwendolyn the winner, is the set that falls from the lottery cage. Let's describe God's action as:

A: God's making it the case that the set of balls S falls from the lottery machine

And we will say that this introduces the following event description:

E: The falling of the set of balls S from the lottery machine

When we say that S fell from the machine for a reason, we are insisting that an action has occurred – that God has made it the case that the set of balls S falls from the lottery machine. But if this is a basic action on God's part, then our claim does not commit us to saying that the event, described as the falling of the set of balls S from the lottery machine, was physically determined to occur, in preference to any other possible outcome.

I see no reason why the outcome of a lottery cannot be a direct or immediate reflection of God's will that a particular set of numbers be drawn, even though a *physical* analysis of the event involved – the falling of the set of balls S from the lottery machine – reveals that this was no more likely to occur than any other outcome. Indeed, traditionally it has been thought that a miracle is an event that lacks a physical cause, which means that it was not determined to occur by any set of physical forces. Yet this has never stood in the way of our wanting to refer it to divine agency; quite to the contrary, it has been thought to facilitate such a claim. True, this has often been thought of in terms of God's supplying some *supernatural* force to produce the event. But if everything we have observed up to now is correct, this part of the story is something that we can discard.

With this in mind, let us give a parallel analysis to God's action in a miracle, such as God's turning water into wine. The act description:

A: God's turning water into wine

introduces the event description:

E: Water's turning into wine

It has traditionally been thought that an event like water's turning into wine cannot be accounted for as the result of physical forces; thus a physical analysis of this event would count it as an anomaly, that is, as an event that is not determined to occur by its physical circumstances. Yet this fact provides no impediment to saying that God acts in turning water into wine. And in particular, there seems to be no conceptual requirement that we think of God as tinkering with physical forces in order to turn water into wine. There had better not be, since as far as we know, there are no physical forces that can bring this about.

What this seems to show is that a divine action may supervene upon an event that is not determined to occur by any set of physical forces. And I would suggest that this conclusion applies to events that represent the outcome of random processes. As far as the selection of lottery balls is concerned, our argument arrives at a rather interesting conclusion, which is that God can make it the case that the set of lottery balls S is selected without 'cheating' in order to bring this about, that is, without manipulating the circumstances so as to determine physically the outcome of the lottery. God's action in making it the case that S is selected is compatible with a physical analysis of the companion event that counts the falling of the lottery balls as the result of a random process.

The Causal Joint

To say that God performs basic actions is to say that there are things that God does, but that God does not do them by doing anything else, and what that implies is that God employs no means in doing them. In describing something as a basic action on the part of God, then, we are saying that there is no description possible of *how* God does these things. This means that an account of these actions must be purely intentional or teleological; we can say *why* God does them – even if we do not know, it makes sense at least to speak of God as having a reason for doing them. But we cannot say *how* God does them, because God employs no means in bringing them about. To ask how God does *x* is to presume that God does *x* by doing something else. In the case of a basic action, however, this presumption is false.

Some philosophers wish to argue, as against this possibility, that a purely intentional (or teleological) account of God's action in the world will not do. To use John Polkinghorne's way of putting the matter, 'we must consider what might be the "causal joint" connecting the whole to its parts, the human self to its body, God to creation' (2003: 58).

Nicholas Saunders takes up the suggestion that we might limit ourselves to describing special divine action in purely intentional terms, as I propose to do here. He considers an example from John Macmurray, who considers the prospect of someone making a trip by automobile to Edinburgh. Macmurray notes:

> I can always ask, 'What happens when I do something?' when I drive a car from Glasgow to Edinburgh, for example. The question refers to all the elements in my action that do themselves, as it were; which are not determined by a deliberate and specific intentions of my own. Consequently a complete account of my journey is possible, which nowhere refers to any intentions of mine . . . We keep within the field of happening by excluding questions which involve a reference to agency. The moment we ask, 'Why were you going to Edinburgh anyway?' the tracing of causal processes or continuant patterns must stop, because the answer must refer to an intention. 'Because I live in Edinburgh', might be a sufficient answer. (1991: 160)

Saunders concedes that 'there is nothing intrinsically wrong in adopting this distinction between natural events and events that occur as a result of some intention . . . Where this distinction is misused, however, is when the focus on the element of intention is pursued to such an extent that the causal aspect to [special divine action] is simply denied' (2002: 32). He responds to Macmurray's claim by suggesting that a complete description of the trip to Edinburgh would answer not only the question 'Why did you visit Edinburgh?' but also the question '*How* did you visit Edinburgh?' (2002: 33). Saunders concludes:

> If we are seeking a coherent understanding of divine action then we simply cannot ignore the causal 'how' questions about God's action. After all, even our purely intentional descriptions of divine action owe much to our understanding and knowledge of God's causal activity in history. So while it may be true that an intentional description of events can give a more *useful* explanation in circumstances such as Macmurray's car journey, it is by no means true that this obviates the need for a causal account of [special divine action]. (2002: 34, original emphasis)

At issue between Macmurray and Saunders is whether an intentional account of the trip to Edinburgh is a complete one. Now of course Macmurray tells us that the intentional account is a sufficient answer to a particular question, namely, 'Why did you go to Edinburgh', and there seems little reason to suppose that the answer, 'Because I live there', is in any sense an incomplete response to that question. Perhaps Saunders merely wants to point out that there are other questions that might be asked of the trip as well, such as 'How did you get there?' One way to pursue the matter would be to invoke standards for completeness by which we do not have a complete account of the trip until *all* of the questions that might be asked about it have been answered – the 'hows' in addition to the 'whys'.

It may be too obvious to bear mentioning, but questions of divine agency are, after all, questions about *agency*, and while I think that there are certainly times at which it bears on someone's agency to indicate how they do what they do, it is equally clear that some attempts to provide a causal account will be exercises in irrelevance.

Suppose Edwin interrupts an important meeting. Perhaps the most obvious question we might ask about his interruption of the meeting is *why* he interrupted it. Did he intend to sabotage the meeting – to prevent the people present from achieving their goal? Was he hankering for attention? Or was he merely trying to communicate an emergency message to one of the participants? The answer to this question may tell us quite a bit about Edwin's action, as well as illuminating his character as an agent. In this example it would also be reasonable to ask *how* Edwin disrupted the meeting; the answer to this question may shed light on the nature of his action. For example, it may be of interest to know whether he interrupted the meeting by quietly handing its moderator a note, or whether he did it by riding into the room on a horse and firing a gun into the ceiling. But we may notice that what makes the 'how' question relevant here is the fact that Edwin interrupted the meeting by *doing something else*, in this case, by riding into the room on a horse and firing a gun into the ceiling. In other words, his interrupting the meeting was not a basic action.

Let us consider instead a basic action on Edwin's part, such as Edwin's raising his arm. The question 'How did Edwin raise his arm?' is motivated by a false presupposition, namely, that he raised his arm by doing something else. But if this is a basic action on Edwin's part, he did not raise his arm by doing anything else; he *just raised it*. In this case the only question that we can ask that treats Edwin's action *as* an action is the 'why' question – 'Why did Edwin raise his arm?'

We can, of course, ask for the causal mechanism responsible for the arm's going up. Here 'the arm's going up' describes an event. But if we now go on to describe the various physiological processes that make it possible for an arm to go up, we are no longer discussing Edwin's agency.

The same may be said of divine actions. I do not see how we can deny that, if God acts at all, then God performs basic actions. Otherwise, as we saw in Chapter 4, we seem committed to an infinite regress; if everything that God does, God does by doing something else, then there is no way for God to *commence* any action. Thus if God acts at all, then we cannot avoid the conclusion that God acts in an unexplained – and unexplainable – direct sense, without the need for any mediating causal interaction.[3] (Cf. Saunders 2002: 39ff.) Any interest in a 'causal joint' – an account of how God influences natural phenomena – must come to a full stop when it encounters God's basic activity. It is not as though there are cogs and levers that God manipulates to bring these things about, but that these mechanisms are forever hidden from our limited human intellects, as Austin Farrer (1967) seems to suggest. Divine basic actions do not *have* any causal mechanism. And lest we think the suggestion is intolerably weird – one is almost tempted to say *supernatural* – let us remember that the same is true of human actions.

Locating Divine Basic Actions: How Far Down Should We Go?

I have defended the possibility of giving a teleological account of miracles as basic actions. I have considered an objection, from the perspective of one who wishes to defend the need to find a 'causal joint' for divine action, that we cannot ignore the question of what means God employs when God acts in the world. The primary result of our discussion so far is that, unless we wish to involve ourselves in an infinite regress, we *must* at some point abandon the search for such a means. But of course a legitimate question arises here. What is the appropriate point at which we ought to abandon the search for the means by which God acts? We have allowed that God may act in a non-basic way, and when God does, then questions about the mechanism of divine actions may be relevant.[4]

We have already considered the possibility that God may fund an orphanage by bringing it about that a particular set of lottery numbers is selected. Another example may be found in God's bringing about the escape of the Israelites from Egypt, which he does by parting the Red Sea; the parting of the sea is something that God does, according to Exodus, by raising a strong wind:[5]

Then Moses stretched out his hand over the sea, and all that night the LORD drove the sea back with a strong east wind and turned it into dry land. The waters were divided, and the Israelites went through the sea on dry ground, with a wall of water on their right and on their left. (Exodus 14.21–22, NIV)

The Egyptians pursue the Israelites and are all drowned when the waters rush back in at Moses' command. There is much here that will be of interest to a theological exegesis; in parting the sea with a strong wind, God is represented as acting through the forces of nature – a force, in particular, associated with the weather. That the Israelites are forced to cross the sea with walls of water on each side is indicative of the trust they must place in God in order to make good their escape from slavery. And the fact that their manner of escape results in the destruction of the Egyptians is surely significant as well, given that 'when the Israelites saw the great power the LORD displayed against the Egyptians, the people feared the LORD and put their trust in him and in Moses his servant' (Exodus 14.31).

Now for reasons that I hope to make clear, I favor treating the description of God as raising the east wind as the description of a basic divine action. I see no reason why an omnipotent being cannot simply *will* that the wind come up to drive back the waters and have it be so, without having to engage in the micro-management of air and water molecules. But we ought to consider an alternative account. A critic might argue here that for all we know, God did not 'just raise' the wind, but God raised the wind by doing something else, e.g. possibly creating a low-pressure area in the neighborhood into which air moved from a higher-pressure region to the east. The question of how God managed to raise the wind is out of order, of course, if this is a basic divine action. But why should we suppose that it is? And of course the problem we face here is that without any reason to suppose that God's creation of a low-pressure area is a basic divine action, we might pursue the matter by asking how God did this. Now I do not claim any expertise in any of the physical sciences, nor in meteorology in particular, but I believe a possible account might be that God may have created the low-pressure area by heating the air near the earth's surface, causing it to rise. I am not sure how the causal story would proceed from here, but I am interested in the possibility that it might somehow trace back to one or more events that are non-deterministic.

Now I confess that I am uncertain just what sort of non-deterministic phenomenon might account for the raising of the east wind and its subsequent efficacy in driving back the water of the Red Sea. Perhaps this might be attributed to the random motion of air and water molecules. Perhaps this could be explained by appeal to quantum phenomena, or perhaps chaos theory might be invoked. In what follows I will speak of the possibility that the parting of the Red Sea rests ultimately on some set of non-determined phenomena or another, and I will call this set of phenomena 'Q'. I will speak of Q as involving the motion of very small particles of one sort or another. Whether we think of this as involving the arrangement of water molecules or whether we think of this in terms of quantum states is not important. I am hoping that what I have to say here will apply equally well to any attempt to locate basic divine agency at the level of micro-processes.

I have the very strong sense that once we start talking about low-pressure areas and non-deterministic micro-events such as molecular motions, we are no longer talking about divine agency. However, my intuition here does not seem to be universally accepted. Some writers insist on the importance of identifying divine agency with non-determined processes. For example, Nancey Murphy, Robert John Russell, and Thomas Tracy favor an appeal to quantum indeterminacy in making this out. Given the potential for controversy here, it seems reasonable to say something about how we ought to go about locating basic divine agency. I wish to argue that it should be at the 'macro' level of ordinary experience; with the example at hand – the parting of the Red Sea – it would be with God's raising the east wind.[6]

Now let us recall, before going any further, that unless we wish to invoke an infinite regress, we must suppose that for any instance of divine agency, there is something that God does as a basic act. Let us consider three candidates for the location of God's basic action.

One possibility is to suggest that God's basic actions take place in a supernatural realm, and that these actions are able to influence natural events. As we have already seen in Chapter 2, this leaves us having to explain how there can be any interaction between the two domains of nature and the supernatural. There will be something that God 'just does' within the realm of the supernatural, and then we will have to account for the causal joint (as it were) between nature and the supernatural. Given the problems that we observed in Chapter 2, I think we should avoid locating divine basic actions on the other side of any supposed boundary between nature and the supernatural.

A better candidate would be to locate God's basic actions at the level of non-determined micro-events of one sort or another. One reason for locating divine basic actions at this level is that, if the movement of fundamental particles is not physically determined, we *cannot* pursue the physical account any further – for the simple reason we have run out of causes. There simply *is* no physical cause that will account for why a particular particle is doing what it is doing, at the time that it is doing it, if its behavior is not physically determined. Furthermore, if it is not determined, there may be any number of states that such a particle might be in that will be consistent with the laws of nature. That means we can say that a particular particle P is in a particular state S because God wants P to be in S. We can find divine agency here, and say that God *makes it the case* that P is in S, and this is consistent with our physical theory because P's being in S is compatible with (i.e. subsumable under) the laws of nature. It gives us a way to explain how God may introduce novelty into the world without interfering in natural processes. This may be a very attractive account to anyone who wants to reconcile divine agency with physical theory.

Associating divine agency with non-determined events may have even greater appeal if we are concerned to defend a conception of special divine agency – that is, to defend the idea that God acts at particular times and at particular places – and particularly if we are worried about making this out in such a way that God's actions are consistent with our physical theory,[7] in the sense that the events to be associated with divine agency (such as the Red Sea's being parted) may be subsumed under the laws of nature.[8]

Divine Manipulation of Microprocesses: An Alternative

I have acknowledged that a problem facing my account is to give some general sense of when we ought to say that God employs a means in acting, and when God does not. I am particularly concerned with the idea that God acts at the level of microprocesses, manipulating these as a means to bring about events on the level of ordinary human experience.

I think that there are several problems that arise when we try to locate divine basic actions at the level of microprocesses. Let me begin, however, by pointing out that if we are concerned with the benefits that this picture of things seems to offer us, we might enjoy these without supposing that God intentionally manipulates 'micro' states in order to influence events at the 'macro' level of ordinary human experience. All that is required of us is that we suppose that divine agency *supervenes upon* these states.

Perhaps an analogy to human action will help us here. Suppose I raise my arm, and I do not raise it by doing anything else, so that my raising it is a basic action on my part. When I raise my arm, an event occurs that may be described as my arm's rising. (We referred to this above as a 'companion event'.) A physical analysis of my arm's rising will no doubt discover that this is really a very complex physiological phenomenon consisting of muscular contractions and neural firings, etc. For all I know, a complete neurological picture of what is happening when my arm rises will include a very detailed picture of myriad quantum states, any one of which might have been otherwise had my arm not gone up. I want to say that my action, in raising my arm, *supervenes upon* this physical mechanism. Yet I do not raise my arm by manipulating neurons or quantum states. My raising of my arm is a basic action, which means that I do not raise it by doing anything else.

Similarly God's basic action, in parting of the Red Sea, might be the raising of the wind. It may also be that the wind's coming up – considered now as a mere event or happening, the companion event to God's raising the wind – may be given a very detailed physical analysis by which it can be described in terms of pressure differentials molecular movements; for all I know it may have its causal origins in the concatenation of various kinds of quantum states. But it does not follow from this that God specifically intends for all of these states to occur. To put the matter somewhat crudely: God may simply intend to raise the wind, and let nature take care of the details.

Peter Van Inwagen gives a discussion that is on point here. Van Inwagen considers the possibility that there might be an infinite number of initial arrangements that would suit God's purposes in creating the world. For the sake of simplicity he considers the possibility that there are just two such states, X and Y. Given that either of these alternatives suits God's purposes equally well, God has no reason to prefer either of them, and so God decrees the disjunction: 'Let there be either X or Y. Suppose then that Y comes into existence. Van Inwagen asserts that in this case 'it is no part of God's plan that Y – as opposed to X – exist, and the result of His decree might just as well have been the existence of X.'[9] (1988: 227ff.). What this suggests is that God's agency might be expressed in the existence of Y without God's *specifically intending* that Y be the case.

The example is particularly relevant if, as seems likely, God's will that the Red Sea part may be multiply realizable, i.e. that it might be realized in any number of different arrangements of matter at the micro level. Particle M1 might have been at location L1, or it might have been at L2 and particle M2 might have been at L1 instead, and so on with all of the particles that are involved. Surely the Red Sea's parting in this particular place and at this particular time might have come about through any one of countless possible combinations of micro-events. Since what God cares about is that the Red Sea part, then God has no reason to be invested in any one of these combinations. There is no reason to suppose that God wills one of them in preference to any other.

Arguments for Divine Basic Actions at the Macro Level

We are considering the problem of determining the level at which God's basic agency ought to be located, and in particular we are considering the question of whether there is a presumption in favor of associating it with non-deterministic phenomena – and particularly with quantum states – or whether we ought to associate them with events at the 'macro' level of ordinary human experience. I have tried to identify what some of the motivations might be to locate basic divine agency at the level of microprocesses; in particular, it allows us a way of explaining how particular instances of divine agency might be thought of as introducing genuine novelty into the world without doing violence to the idea that every event in nature may be subsumed under the laws of nature. However, I have argued that we may enjoy these benefits without having to say that God acts in a basic way at the subatomic level. These benefits may accrue to an account of divine agency by which God's basic actions are placed at the level of ordinary experience. Thus a concern with lawful divine special agency is served equally well by the account I will offer here.

I will now proceed to give specific arguments against the presumption that God acts basically at the subatomic level,[10] and for supposing that at least in the usual case, God's basic actions are at the level of ordinary experience. There are a number of reasons why, in the absence of any strong positive argument in favor of God's micromanagement of physical states, we should decide against this picture of things.

(1) First, the assumption of divine micromanagement unnecessarily complicates our picture of God's intentions. That is, I would suggest an Ockhamist principle of parsimony here, dictating that we not ascribe more intentions to God than we must, in order to give a personal (or teleological) account of an event occurring at the level of ordinary experience. Now the text of Exodus says that God raised the east wind, and so we are committed to viewing the raising of the wind as an instance of divine agency. There is nothing in Exodus, however, that suggests that we must pursue the matter any further, and so in the absence of any other reason for supposing that God specifically intended each of the microprocesses on

which this occurrence supervenes, we should refrain from trying to locate God's intentionality at a lower level.

(2) We have already noticed that God's raising of the east wind is a phenomenon that can be realized in more than one way, i.e. it is multiply realizable. For example, God might have moved particle M1 to location L1, or God might have moved it to L2 and placed particle M2 at L1 instead. But if this is the case then God cannot have any reason for moving M1 to L1 instead of putting it some-place else, and if we understand God to be specifically intending this particular move, then we must understand God as making the choice arbitrarily – by flipping a mental coin, as Peter Van Inwagen describes it. Van Inwagen suggests that such a supposition is incon-sistent with the divine nature, and I agree (1988: 228ff.). Indeed if God has no reason to move M1 to L1 instead of moving it to some other location, we might well wonder whether this would even con-stitute a divine action, if actions are things that are done for a reason. God *has* no reason to move M1 to L1 instead of putting it elsewhere, as long as the sea gets parted.

(3) Supposing that God did specifically intend all of the micro-events that made it possible for the Red Sea to part, this fact seems to shed little light on the nature of God's agency. That is, saying that God intentionally moved M1 to L1 tells us nothing about the char-acter of God's action, nothing about the nature of God as an agent, and nothing about the nature of God's relationship to humanity. Contrast this with the observations we made above about God's parting the sea by means of a strong wind; here the means employed by God reveal something of God's nature. Surely it is concerns such as these that should be the focus of a theological account. I am at a loss to find anything of any theological signif-icance in M1's being at L1 rather than somewhere else.

(4) Furthermore, if what I have said above is correct, and God would have to make an arbitrary choice regarding where to move each molecule, then speaking of these as divine actions *cannot* tell us anything about God as a rational agent. Our actions, and our character, are only intelligible to the extent that we are seen as having reasons for what we do, and an arbitrary choice is not one that is governed by reason.

(5) The criteria that we use to identify instances of divine agency ought to be in conformity with religious life and practice. For example, prayer is an important part of a theistic religious practice, and within that practice, a divine action is something that is understood as being something we might pray that God will do – or it might be something that we would pray that God will *not* do. An Israelite might pray that God free her from bondage; she might pray that God save her from the pursuing Egyptians. When she is safe on the other side of the water and the Egyptian army is destroyed, she may thank God for saving her. Even if she knows something about the microprocesses involved in the parting of the Red Sea, she does not pray that God will move particle M1 to location L1 and so on; there simply does not appear to be any reason, from *within* a theistic religious practice, to locate basic divine actions at the microlevel. And, I wish to argue, theology should individuate divine actions in a manner that can connect fruitfully with religious life and practice.

It may be that all instances of divine agency supervene on non-deterministic phenomena. When someone is suddenly cured of a terrible disease, this may well be accounted for as the result of an unlikely concatenation of myriad non-deterministic events, such as quantum states, etc. But one does not pray for a quantum state. One prays for a *cure*. To the extent that a divine action is seen as a response to prayer, or to human needs generally, it must then be the cure that is the primary locus of divine agency; that is to say, the basic or primitive assignment of divine agency is given in the description, 'God cured the disease'.

It is true, of course, that one may pray for a cure, and God may supply the cure by engaging in the intentional manipulation of countless micro-events in order to produce the cure. But there does not seem to be any reason for supposing that God acts in this way. God can will that someone be cured without willing the specific circumstances in which the cure manifests itself. Unless we have a particular reason for thinking that God is acting at this level, my suggestion is that our discourse regarding divine agency remain closely connected with concrete practices in religious life such as prayer, praise, and thanksgiving. If our relationship with God is conducted on the 'macro' level of ordinary experience, then absent good reasons to the contrary, our primitive assignments of divine agency should be at the level of ordinary experience as well.

(6) Finally, it simply does not seem as though we have anything to gain by trying to place divine agency at the level of micro-processes. Those who look for divine action at this level are often in search of a 'causal joint' between a transcendent God and natural processes. Suppose we say that God does individually manipulate such microprocesses, placing particle M1 at location L1 and so on. We now have an action description, 'God placed M1 at L1'. How does this help us with the causal joint problem? We have been speaking of this movement as non-determined. What this means, of course, is that it is not determined to occur by any physical force. If the causal joint, or the point of God's supposed interaction with physical processes, must be identified with some physical force, then the search for the causal joint must end here, and we *still* do not know what connects the transcendent God to physical events. The alternative, it would seem, is to continue the search by trying to find a *supernatural* cause for the movement of M1 to L1. We might say that this movement is the result of an interaction between M1 and some supernatural force, and try to locate the causal joint at the point of this interaction. In this case our commitment to the existence of a causal joint is a commitment to supernaturalism, and it brings with it the difficulties that I tried to describe in the first three chapters above.

The alternative, of course, is to say that God's placement of M1 at location L1 is a basic divine action – something that God does without employing any means or mechanism in doing it. This means that the search for a causal joint has come to an end in any case. So what, then, is the advantage of chasing it down to the level of microprocesses?

The point of all this is simply that, if there is no reason to suppose that God specifically intends each and every micro-state on which God's actions supervene, then there is no reason to suppose that an inquiry into these micro-states will reveal anything of the Divine Nature, or of God's relationship to humanity. Most assuredly, such an inquiry might be quite useful in advancing the cause of science. However, it has little to offer theology.

Quantum Gaps and Special Divine Agency

I want to consider a final objection to my account, which continues in the spirit of insisting that we must give a causal analysis of divine action. It is one that has been made against an account that is similar to my own – namely, one defended by John Compton, who seeks to show that, because we may describe human beings as acting without assuming that there is no scientific explanation for human bodily movements, so too divine agency does not require that we find gaps in the natural order. Thomas Tracy has criticized Compton's account, arguing that in order for God to engage in special actions – i.e. to act in particular places and at particular times and for particular reasons – we must locate God's agency in some form of 'gappy' phenomenon. I am prepared to admit the possibility that, in order for God to engage in special agency, there may have to be processes in nature that are not determined. However, I wish to deny that this implies that God acts within the gaps that we may find in nature; it is sufficient that we acknowledge that divine actions *supervene* on non-determined phenomena.

Compton observes that when he moves his arm,

> This movement is a succession of *events* linked together causally in my body. These events may be described and explained as completely as is desired. And yet, from the agent's point of view (my view) or from yours, this happening constitutes not merely a series of movements or specific bodily events, but an *action* . . . What is most instructive, my arm motion is an action *at the same time*, if not in the same respect, in which it is a succession of causally linked events. Between these two perspectives there is no conflict whatsoever. (1972: 37, original emphasis)

Compton hopes to draw out the analogy in speaking of the relation of God to the world, suggesting that 'we can distinguish the causal development of events from the meaning of these events viewed as God's action . . . God [does not] need to find a "gap" in nature in order to act, any more than you or I need a similar interstice in our body chemistry' (1972: 39).

Thomas Tracy offers qualified praise for Compton's approach:

> This opens up some promising possibilities in theology. Just as efficient-causal and intentional-teleological vocabularies offer distinct and non-competing ways of talking about human beings, so too will these vocabularies both be available in describing the world around us. We can regard events as belonging to a law governed natural order and also as enacting God's intentions. This frees theology from any need to claim that events which the faithful have come to regard as special divine actions must necessarily, on the physical level, lie beyond the scope of adequate scientific explanation. (2000: 308)

I share Tracy's interest in an account that frees theology from the need to claim that special divine actions – particular acts done at particular times in response to particular human needs – lie beyond the scope of any adequate scientific explanation. It is my claim that we can say that even the occurrence of a miracle – as an instance of special divine agency – need not imply the inadequacy of the natural sciences. However, Tracy is skeptical about whether the analogy of human and divine action can accomplish this task, at least insofar as Compton makes this out. Tracy sees problems arising in connection with Compton's embrace of the view that human mental states are realized in brain states. Tracy writes:

> In the first place, positions of this sort directly link physiological and intentional descriptions of action; indeed, the latter depend upon the former. Understood this way, Compton's analysis of human action no longer provides a conceptual model that releases us from puzzling over the relation between descriptions of events as divine actions and scientific descriptions of the causal order of the world. And, in the second place, action theories of this type are thoroughly deterministic, though they may be coupled with compatibilist position on human freedom.

If this is taken over into theology, Compton's position will reduce to . . . a divine determinism in which, after the initial creative act, every event will be an indirect act of God, but no event will be a direct divine act in history . . .

If by an 'act of God in history' we mean a direct divine init- iative (beyond creation and conservation) that affects the course of events in the world, then it is at least very difficult to see how such an action could leave a closed causal structure untouched. (2000: 310)

Now if we are not so concerned about accounting for the pos- sibility of special divine actions, we might instead understand divine agency as Gordon Kaufman does,[11] in terms of the complex 'master act' of God, which is the 'temporal movement of all nature and history toward the realization of his original intention in creation' (1972: 142). Tracy argues that 'if God acts only to initiate and sustain the world, then God cannot respond to our actions . . . [and thus] only created free agents will make any novel contribution to the direction of history' (2000: 304). I think Tracy is right to be concerned about this. Theistic religious practice presumes God to be actively involved with the world – not just anticipating our needs from some time in the remote past, but responding to them in the present, as they arise. Saying how this is possible is particularly important to any account of miracles.

The question before us, then, is whether Compton's original goal can be achieved in a manner consistent with the view that God engages in special acts. We understand that to assume I act when I raise my arm does not require us to eliminate the possibility that there is a natural explanation for the companion event that we may describe as my arm's rising. Compton's claim is that to suppose I act, when I raise my arm, does not require us to assume that there is any 'gap' in the physiological description of this event. Can we understand divine agency in analogous terms? Or must we, as Tracy insists, give some account of 'the relation between descriptions of events as divine actions and scientific descriptions of the causal order of the world'? (2000: 310). In particular, must we, as Tracy suggests, embrace some picture of the world as 'causally open' –

supposing, for example, that 'God may act in history . . . by determining at least some events at the quantum level'? (2000: 318).

Let me address Tracy's concerns over Compton's account in
reverse order. First, let us consider his worry concerning Compton's
apparent determinism. It may well be that special divine agency is
impossible in a deterministic universe.[12] In such a case Tracy
suggests that the only novelty that may be introduced into the
universe is through the actions of free creatures, such as human
beings. But of course one may argue that if the universe is deterministic, then even human beings will be incapable of introducing
any real novelty into the world, since their actions will be determined by antecedent conditions. It is interesting to reflect on the
possibility that the requirements for special divine agency may be
the same as those for libertarian agency on the part of human
beings.

Let us assume, for the sake of argument, the truth of the plausible claim that special divine agency will be impossible on a deterministic picture of the universe. In this case, the problem with
Compton's account is not with the possibility of making an analogy
between human and divine agency, but with the consequences for
that analogy if our model of human agency is deterministic.[13] It
would seem therefore that, at most, all we need to acknowledge on
this point is that, for the analogy to go through, we must adopt
some form of libertarian account of human agency. (My guess is
that few theologians will be disturbed by this prospect.) However we
make out the possibility of free human agency, if we are to maintain
the analogy between human and divine agency, it will have to be
possible to carry the story over to our account of God's special
actions.

Now let us consider the other issue that Tracy raised. Must we
give some account of the relation between divine action descriptions and event descriptions? Surely in the case of human agency,
our ability to describe someone as raising her hand (an action
description) does not require us to give a physical analysis of the
companion event of her arm's going up.[14] Why, then, should we
presume that our description of something as an instance of divine
agency requires us to give a physical analysis of the accompanying

event? I see no reason why, without further argument, we should suppose that there is a general requirement on divine agency that does not exist in the case of human action.

I suspect that what Tracy has in mind is that, if God is to engage in special agency, then we must be able to identify God's agency in some way with particular kinds of physical events, and in particular, with non-deterministic events, such as those occurring at the quantum level. If this is Tracy's concern then there appears to be a connection between these two issues; that is, his concern with the relation between divine act descriptions and event descriptions *is* in essence a concern to connect the possibility of special divine agency with a non-deterministic picture of the world.

Now one way to solve the problem here is to correlate divine actions descriptions directly with non-deterministic event descriptions. Thus we may say that God acts in making it the case that T occurs, and the companion event, the occurrence of T, is to be understood as a non-determined event occurring at the quantum level. I do not, however, see that it is necessary to correlate action descriptions with event descriptions in this way. We may grant that special divine agency requires nature to be non-deterministic in some way without saying that God intentionally manipulates non-determined events. The alternative is to say that God's agency supervenes on these events.

Suppose that both special divine agency, and free human agency, are only possible in a non-determined universe; suppose in addition that the universe is in fact non-determined, and that this is due to the fact that the phenomena of ordinary experience are somehow rooted in the occurrence of certain kinds of non-determined quantum states. Now suppose that I act in a basic way by raising my hand. This act will be accompanied by a companion event, namely, my hand's rising. If free agency requires quantum indeterminacy, and I have acted *freely* in raising my hand, when I raise it, then non-determined events must be occurring somewhere, presumably in my brain. But I do not raise my hand *by* seeing to it that these events come about. Their occurrence may be metaphysically necessary if my raising my hand is to qualify as an instance of free agency, but this does not mean that I bring these events about as a means in raising it. It may be a metaphysical implication of the fact that I have raised my hand *freely* that my action supervenes on some form of non-determined phenomena. But the only event description that is logically implied by saying that I acted in raising my hand is that *my hand rose.*

Suppose now that God acts, in a basic way, by curing Sally of some terrible disease. On our supposition, this is only an instance of special divine agency if some form of non-determined events, for example, events occurring at the quantum level, are involved with the remission of Sally's illness. Thus it may be a metaphysical implication, *of the assumption that this is a special divine action*, that the physical processes by which Sally's being cured manifested itself are connected in some way with non-deterministic phenomena such as quantum states. But this does not mean that God brought about those quantum states in order to cure Sally. Strictly speaking, all that is implied by describing God as acting, in curing Sally, is that an event occurred which may be described as *Sally's becoming cured.* And of course the point here is that there is nothing standing in the way of our describing God's curing Sally as a basic action.

I would make a final observation, which is that none of this requires us to think of the universe as *causally open*, at least if that is taken to mean that it is subject to some form of non-physical influence. Scientific theories that countenance the occurrence of non-determined phenomena are content to leave them undetermined – which I take to imply causal closure. And I think we should say that if, for example, God acts by curing Sally of her disease, and that Sally's being cured manifests itself, at a primitive physical level, in the occurrence of various non-deterministic phenomena, we do not have to think of God as acting within the gaps of these phenomena to effect Sally's cure. We may think of these micro-events as simply *occurring*, that is, we may think of them as mere events rather than as divine actions.

My conclusion, then, is that an analogy between human and divine agency *can* accomplish the goals that appear to have motivated Compton, and which Tracy seems to approve. If theology wishes to describe the world in teleological terms, by speaking of God as active in the world, it may do this in a way that does not bring it into conflict with the way in which the natural sciences describe the world. I have allowed for the possibility that the universe must be non-deterministic if God is to engage in special agency, as opposed to God's acting only by creating and sustaining the universe. But this is consistent with the scientific picture of the world, and this possibility does not trouble the analogy between human and divine agency, particularly given the plausible assumption that human free agency has a similar requirement.

I have attempted in this chapter to respond to some objections that might be made to my account of miracles as divine basic actions. The focus in this chapter has been, not so much on the nature of miracles *per se*, but on the broader question of basic divine agency. We began by considering the suggestion that the sort of analogy I wish to make between divine and basic actions requires viewing the world as God's body. I have argued here that we need not defend the view that the world is God's body in order to speak of God as acting in the world in a basic way. An agent may act in a basic way in moving things other than her body, as may occur, for example, in cases of psychokinesis.

I then considered the suggestion that we cannot avoid giving a causal account of how God acts in the world. Such a suggestion seems to insist on treating divine agency as non-basic. I have acknowledged that some divine actions seem to be non-basic, and that a discussion of how God brings them about may be theologically illuminating. However, I have also tried to show that this will not always be the case. In particular, an attempt to locate divine agency at the level of micro-phenomena does not seem to advance any theological concern over God's nature and purposes. I then offered several arguments for why we should, in the absence of special considerations to the contrary, locate God's basic agency at the level of ordinary experience.

Finally, I considered an objection by Thomas Tracy against an account, defended by John Compton, that is similar to the one I have developed here. Tracy argued that the analogy between human and divine action, as Compton makes it out, cannot account for the possibility of special divine agency. Furthermore, he argued, we cannot avoid saying how it is that divine action descriptions connect up with event descriptions; his suggestion is that we associate divine action descriptions with the description of events occurring at the subatomic level. In response I have attempted to show that the analogy between human and divine agency can accommodate the requirements for special divine agency, and I attempted to provide reinforcement for my arguments in the previous section that this does not require us to speak of God as acting at the subatomic level.

Chapter 6

A Context for Miracles

In the present work I have argued at some length against a super-naturalistic conception of the miraculous. It is important to this conception that a miracle be understood as lacking any natural cause, and lacking as well a natural explanation; these deficiencies are thought to show that a miracle can only be accounted for as having a supernatural cause. In Chapters 1–3 of this work I tried to show the liabilities of the supernaturalist account. In Chapter 4 I commenced my defense of a teleological account of the mirac-ulous, arguing that a miracle may be understood as a basic action on the part of God. Such an understanding frees us from the need to speak of God as the *cause* of a miracle, and thus represents an alternative to supernaturalism.

I have tried to make clear how it is that we may hope to make a miracle intelligible by referring it to divine agency. What is important is to understand the difference between the kind of intelligibility that theistic religion brings to a miracle, and the sort of intelligibility that is offered by a scientific explanation. I have urged a conception of the miraculous by which a miracle is seen as something that happens for a reason, and which tries to articulate its significance for human life. These concerns lie well beyond the boundary of the natural sciences. Such explanations, if we wish to refer to them as such, are not in competition with those provided by the sciences.

In this chapter I hope to build on the teleological account that I commenced in the last one. My particular emphasis here will be to show how we might identify (or recognize) an event as miracu-lous without inquiring into whether it has a natural cause. Now it may be objected that the terms 'identify' and 'recognize' are success words. If this is correct, then we cannot identify an event as miraculous unless it *really is* a miracle; thus to speak of identifying a miracle is to assume that miracles really do occur. I have not, of course, offered any argument for this. I have not sought to operate from the position of the apologist, who wishes to give us reason to believe that God exists and is active in the world – and who may hope to give criteria for the miraculous by which the occurrence of a miracle would be evidence for these propositions. Rather, I have been concerned to start from the position of theistic religion, in which the reality of God, and of God's activity in the world, are not in question. I want to show how the term 'miracle' may be applied to events in the world within the context of a theistic religious practice. In any case my concern here may be taken as hypothetical; supposing that we assume the reality of God and the possibility that God acts in the world, what criteria would govern our application of the notions of divine agency generally, and of the miraculous, as a special case of divine agency, to our experience of the world?

It is my argument that in order to qualify as a miracle, an event must be extraordinary, and it must express divine agency; its constituting an action on the part of God will be instrumental to its being significant within the context of theistic religion. By 'extraordinary' I mean, specifically, that the event must be inconsistent with any reasonable expectations we might have had. This may mean that it is inconsistent with our understanding of natural law, but it need not mean this. A particularly surprising coincidence may qualify.

I will be concerned in this chapter to offer a model for determining when an event expresses divine agency: We may say that God's agency is expressed in x when God is *duly thankable* for the occurrence of x – i.e. when thanks are due to God for it. The thankability criterion is implicit in R. F. Holland's discussion of coincidence (or 'contingency') miracles, and has been developed by J. Kellenberger as a sufficient condition for the occurrence of a miracle. I do not agree with Kellenberger that thankability is sufficient for the miraculous – as a criterion for the miraculous, this is much too broad. Surely within theistic religious practice, we may thank God for any number of things that are not miracles. It does seem to me, however, that if God is *duly thankable* for x – i.e. if thanks are due, or owed, to God for x – this implies at least that x is an instance of divine agency. Since I wish to say that divine agency is necessary to something's being a miracle, at least within the context of a theistic religious practice, then due thankability becomes relevant to the task of identifying miracles. I will be particularly interested to show how the thankability criterion works in the identification of miracles without involving any reference to supernatural causes.

I will also defend the thankability criterion against the objection, posed by Nicholas Saunders, that it is subjective, and has no ontological implications vis-à-vis the existence of God.

I hope as well, in this chapter, to discuss – and to defend – the concept of a religiously significant coincidence as a miracle. My motive for this centers on the fact that I am trying to show that a miracle may be consistent with natural law; such 'lawful miracles' would be, in essence, coincidence miracles; they would be events that have natural explanations, and yet are nevertheless significant within the context of theistic religion. What matters, in our search for criteria by which the term 'miracle' may be applied to events in the world, is not whether an event might have a natural explanation. What matters is that it is significant, or meaningful, within the context of a theistic religious practice. Thus my account of miracles, as I will continue to develop it in this chapter, will be seen as a *contextual* one; that is, I want to argue that what makes an event miraculous is, in part, the possibility of integrating it into a religious practice of some kind.

In defending the claim that a miracle may be a religiously significant coincidence – that is, an event that has a natural explanation – I want to pay special attention to a particularly potent objection to this claim. The problem is that if an event has a natural explanation, then the critic is in a position to argue that it would have occurred regardless of God's intentions. I will develop this objection as suggesting that instances of God's agency must satisfy a counterfactual: in order to identify x as a miracle, we must be able to say that x would not have occurred had it not been for God's intention that x occur. I will conclude this chapter by arguing that divine agency can satisfy this counterfactual even in the case of an event that has a natural explanation, which is to say, that it may be satisfied by a religiously significant coincidence.

Thankability and the Miraculous

It is time we paid a little attention to the possibility of identifying miracles. By this I mean, we ought to inquire what sort of criteria might be employed by the practitioner of theistic religion – someone who does not question the reality of God or the possibility of God's acting in miraculous ways – to distinguish miraculous from non-miraculous events.

J. Kellenberger has argued that thankability is a sufficient condition for the miraculous; that is, he suggests that if God may be thanked for the occurrence of some event E, then E is a miracle. He is influenced in this conviction by R. F. Holland's discussion of contingency (or 'coincidence') miracles (1965). Let us begin by considering Holland's example.

Holland imagines that a small child, playing in his toy motor-car, has become stuck on a train track. A train is speeding toward him, but it is on the other side of a curve, and will not be able to see the child until it is too late to stop. The child is preoccupied with trying to free his car from the tracks, which he is unable to do. The child's mother is in a panic. Then, unexpectedly, the train comes to a stop; the engineer has fainted and released his grip on the control lever, causing the train to stop automatically. The child is saved, against all expectations to the contrary, and his mother thanks God for his life. She never ceases to think of the event as a miracle even after finding out the cause for the train's stopping.

Now of course, when the child's mother thanks God for saving her child, it is because she thinks of this as something *done* by God; it is implicit in her thanking God that she conceives the stopping of the train to be a divine action. But she does not do this after first eliminating the possibility that the stopping of the train has a natural cause, and indeed, as Holland draws out the example (1965: 43), she continues to think of the event as a miracle even after coming to an understanding of how the train came to a stop – its 'natural history', as it were.

The fact that the train stopped when it did might be described as a coincidence, by virtue of the fact that the cause of its stopping – the fainting of the engineer – is not linked by any series of natural causes to the child's being stuck on the track.[1] But, unlike the coincidence between the rise of the Ming dynasty and the arrival of the dynasty of Lancaster, the stopping of the train is, Holland tells us, impressive and significant. What accounts for this significance? Holland says:

> The significance of some coincidences as opposed to others arises from their relation to human needs and hopes and fears, their effects for good or ill upon our lives. So we speak of our luck (fortune, fate, etc.). And the kind of thing that, outside religion, we call luck is in religious parlance the grace of God or a miracle of God. But while the reference is the same, the meaning is different. The meaning is different in that whatever happens by God's grace or by a miracle is something for which God is thanked or thankable, something which has been or could be prayed for, something which can be regarded with awe and taken as a sign or made the subject of a vow (e.g. to go on a pilgrimage), all of which can only take place against the background of a religious tradition. (1965: 44)

It is also important to notice that the stopping of the train is something that could not be predicted; indeed its occurrence was contrary to any reasonable prediction that might have been made in the circumstances. Thus it qualifies as extraordinary. And surely its extraordinariness is part of what makes it so impressive.

There are two features present in Holland's discussion of this event that merit special attention. First, a very important element in the mother's identification of this as an action on the part of God is that she understands it as occurring in response to the needs of her child. Of course viewed from this perspective, the stopping of the train is no coincidence at all; the child's mother sees it as *connected* in an important way with the child's situation, with the urgency of his need. To see the stopping of the train in this light is to see it as something that has happened for a *reason*; it is, in short, to view it *teleologically*.

Second, it is a *religiously significant* coincidence, which means that it has a place within theistic religious practice. It is the kind of event that might be prayed for; we can imagine the mother taking a vow, or going on a pilgrimage, as an expression of her gratitude for God's having saved her child. It is important to the theistic conception of a miracle that the occurrence of such an event may play a role in the religious life of the believer.

It is important to recognize the contextual elements here. First, if an event has no significance in regard to anyone's religious practice, there is no reason to describe it as a miracle. There is no miracle in the fact that the dynasty of Lancaster arose at the same time as the Ming dynasty in China, not only because there is nothing particularly surprising about this, but because it has no religious significance. Even if an event were quite extraordinary, if it lacks the capacity to play some role in a religious practice, it can be no more than what Holland has referred to as a *lusus naturae*, or 'sport of nature' (1989); it would be at most a *mere anomaly*.

It is also important to see that the stopping of the train must bear some relationship to human interests – in this case, to the needs of the child and his mother.[2] Indeed, this is surely tied to the religious significance of the event. An event that has no connection to the interests of any being capable of engaging in religious practice would not be a miracle, no matter how extraordinary it might be. We cannot speak of miracles apart from human interests, nor can we speak of them apart from the possibility of making them a part of the relationship between God and humanity.

In some ways the attribution of divine agency to the stopping of the train is like ordinary attributions of agency, i.e. to human beings, and in other respects it is not. One point of comparison is that in the usual case, we do not determine that a human bodily movement is an action, or something done for a reason, by first eliminating the possibility that an explanation can be given for it by reference to neural firings and the like; indeed were we to stop to think about the matter, we might assume that it *does* have such a cause. Thus when I am introduced to Howard and he sticks out his hand, I immediately see that he has done this for a reason, without inquiring as to whether there is a physical explanation for his movement. This is not something that must be settled in order to understand that his movement is purposeful. What allows us to do this is our understanding of the context in which his movement occurs. In this particular case, what is relevant is the fact that we have just been introduced, and that in such a circumstance, given the culture in which we participate, it is appropriate to offer one's hand for shaking. In this particular example, it is a social convention that helps us to recognize the purpose behind Howard's bodily movement.

The point here is reminiscent of Wittgenstein's reference to a miracle as a *gesture* on the part of God. Here is the quote once again:

A miracle is, as it were, a gesture that God makes. As a man sits quietly and then makes an impressive gesture, God lets the world run on smoothly and then accompanies the words of a saint by a symbolic occurrence, a gesture of nature. It would be an instance if, when a saint has spoken, the trees around him bowed, as if in reverence. (1980: 45e)

In referring to a miracle as a gesture, Wittgenstein wants to draw attention to its significance, which he refers to as symbolic – in his example, when we see the trees apparently bowing, we observe them as appearing to manifest a conventional form of behavior that, within the context of certain human cultures, generally expresses purposeful activity.

Of course we are able to see that people are acting for a purpose even when this kind of convention is not operating. If I fall out of my canoe, Howard may stretch out his hand toward me, and I see that he is offering me help in getting out of the water. What enables me to see that this is what he is doing is my understanding of the circumstances (or the context) in which the movement of his arm occurs. In particular, it is significant in this case that I am in need of help, and that Howard's reaching out to me is sufficient to provide that help; it is a response to my need.

Something very similar is operating in the case of Holland's train. The fact that the child's mother sees the train as stopping for a reason comes from her understanding of the circumstances or context; she sees the predicament of her child and is aware of his need. The train stops, the child is saved, and the mother thanks God; implicit in her thanking God is the fact that she sees the stopping of the train as a divine response to the need of her son, and she continues to do so after finding out that the train stopped because the engineer fainted.

Kellenberger draws attention to the fact that the mother continues to thank God for the stopping of the train, and continues to think of it as a miracle even after finding out why the engineer fainted.

> The observation that she could do so is more than a psychological observation on Holland's part. In fact, he draws our attention to a signal conceptual point about the miraculous. The mother can appropriately continue to thank God just so long as she sees the event as a miracle. That is, a conceptual test for the miraculous is the thankability of God. (1979: 155)

The mother can appropriately thank God so long as she sees the event as a miracle, which of course involves seeing it as an act of God; it is clear that a condition of appropriate thankability is that the thanking party believe in God, for Kellenberger tells us that an atheist cannot appropriately thank God for anything owing to the fact that, on his view, there is no being to whom thanks are due. He continues:

> Let me elaborate this point. It has two elements, which should be distinguished. First, a person can appropriately thank God for an occurrence just so long as he sees it as an act of God or due to God's agency, that is, a miracle. Second, God is thankable just for those events that are miracles. If a person appropriately thanks God, if he sincerely thanks God for the occurrence of an event, it does not follow that the event is a miracle; although it does follow that he sees it as a miracle. While if God is thankable for

an event in the sense that thanks are due to Him, then it does follow that the event is a miracle. (1979: 156)

Thankability and the Subjective: An Objection

Nicholas Saunders has complained that Kellenberger's thankability criterion for the miraculous is highly subjective, and devoid of any ontological significance (2002: 51ff.). However, it is important to notice that Kellenberger distinguishes two senses in which God might be thankable for the occurrence of some event E. God is *appropriately* thankable for E when the thanking party believes that God exists and is responsible for the occurrence of E. When Kellenberger makes this claim he seems intent on bringing out an important conceptual point: To *conceive* of God as being thankable for E involves thinking of God as both real and responsible for the occurrence of E.

Kellenberger does not, however, tell us that appropriate thankability is a sufficient condition for the miraculous; indeed in the quote above he explicitly denies this – he says that it does not follow from the fact that I appropriately thank God for the occurrence of an event that it really is a miracle; the only thing that follows is that I see it as a miracle or that I conceive it to be one. Kellenberger is here drawing attention to the conceptual truth – that conceiving of God as thankable for an event implies that I conceive it to be an instance of divine agency.

The sufficient test that Kellenberger offers for the occurrence of a miracle is simply *thankability,* and perhaps the most charitable way to understand what Kellenberger is saying here is that if God is *actually* thankable for E, then E is a miracle. It might be appropriate for me to thank God for E when I believe that God exists and that God is responsible for E – what seems to be at stake here is simply the conditions under which I may *sincerely* thank God. But I might thank God, with all sincerity, for the occurrence of E even though God is not in fact thankable for it, either because God does not exist or because, even if God does exist, E is not something that may correctly be attributed to God's agency.

Due Thankability

It might help to clear up the confusion here if we identify Kellenberger's thankability criterion with those situations in which thanks are *due* to God. Thanks are due to God for the occurrence of *E* only if God really does exist and *E* really is an instance of God's agency. If God really is responsible for saving the child from being run over by Holland's train, then thanks are due to God regardless of how the mother sees things. Even if she were an atheist, we might still say that she *owes* thanks to God or that she *ought* to thank God.

This is an important point and deserves emphasis. We may be tempted, as Saunders appears to be, to suppose that an objective criterion for the miraculous must be a *causal* one. But we see that this is not true. We may say that thanks are due to God for an event without invoking the language of causation; the truth of our claim will, in this case, be independent of anyone's attitudes about the matter, and thus not subjective; furthermore it has clear ontological implications.

Now I think Kellenberger goes too far in making 'due thankability' a sufficient condition for the miraculous; the believer may thank God for her supper but, if it got to her table in the usual way, its presence there would not be a miracle. To speak otherwise seems to run strongly counter to the ordinary usage of the term 'miracle'. The usual sense of 'miracle' requires a miracle to be extraordinary in some way – striking and impressive because its occurrence is contrary to any reasonable expectation we might have had. Of course, as Holland notes, this kind of extraordinariness does not require us to defend a conception of the miraculous as being contrary to natural law. The stopping of Holland's train is quite at odds with our expectations, yet has a natural explanation.

Due Thankability and Apologetic

I am defending the claim that due thankability is a sufficient condition for divine agency. I have argued that, contrary to J. Kellenberger, it is not a sufficient condition for the miraculous; to be a miracle, something more is needed, which is that the occurrence of an event must be contrary to any reasonable expectation that we might have had under the circumstances. This might, of course, mean that we do not see how the event can be subsumed under natural law, but it need not be restricted to such cases. The stopping of Holland's train, contrary to any reasonable expectation we might have given the physical circumstances of the event, qualifies despite its being susceptible to a natural explanation. It applies as well to cases in which someone is cured of a terrible disease, against all reasonable expectations that they will succumb to it, particularly where this occurs in a religiously significant setting, e.g. someone prays to a saint or to a candidate for saint-hood, performs a religious ritual, or hangs a religious medallion around the patient's neck, etc.

The question may now arise, what are the criteria for due thank-ability? I will not attempt to set out, with any rigor, a set of necessary and sufficient conditions for this. But it is important – really *crucial* – to emphasize that this is a matter to be determined within the context of theistic religious practice, in which the existence of God, and God's involvement in the world, are already taken for granted. I have no hope of establishing religiously neutral grounds for due thankability, such as might be embodied in a physical description of an event, with the hope of persuading an atheist that some event satisfies the criteria for due thankability, and therefore that God exists and is active in the world. I have no response to the atheistic skeptic who denies that God is duly thankable for the occurrence of any event. Accordingly, I think there is little apologetic potential in any appeal to due thankability.

That said, it remains for us to ask: For what sort of thing is God normally thanked by the practitioners of theistic religion? And when we consider the matter we see that there are a great many things for which God is commonly thanked. One may, for example, thank God for anything that might be prayed for; the health and safety of oneself or one's friends and family, the good of one's nation, and so on. It is commonplace for theists to thank God in prayer for their meal. To give thanks to God for any of these things is at once to acknowledge that they satisfy a human need and also to acknowledge God's agency in providing them. Significantly, the believer does not typically worry much about whether there is a natural explanation for whatever state of affairs it is that she conceives God as providing; knowing that the food on her table came to be there by entirely natural means does not in the least inhibit her from thanking God for its presence. This kind of thanksgiving is fundamental to theistic practice, and indicates a similarly fundamental conception of divine agency.

This point deserves emphasis. If thankability is to serve as a properly religious criterion for divine action, it must have a role within theistic religious practice and we should expect it to be connected with other elements of that practice, such as prayer. If there is to be a test for due thankability, it should be: Is this the sort of thing for which the theist might pray? Is it the sort of event which might prompt us to undertake a pilgrimage? Trying to determine whether we ought to thank God for the occurrence of an event should not send us looking to see whether it has a natural cause.

Now it may be observed that the criterion of due thankability for divine agency attributes a great many events to God's activity. As Kellenberger points out (1979: 157) we may, within the context of a theistic religious practice, thank God for many things during the course of a normal day. God may be thanked for putting food on the table, for the birth of a child, for a new job or a promotion. I do not see any problem with this; indeed it seems to me that the practitioner of theistic religion really does want to say that God is active in many of the circumstances of her life. But this need not involve proliferating miracles, since not every instance of divine agency must qualify as miraculous. We will not, however, be in danger of excessively multiplying miracles if we restrict the use of the term 'miracle' to events that are extraordinary, in the sense that they are contrary to what we might reasonably have expected to occur. And once again, as I have already pointed out, this may include events that we are unable to subsume under any form of natural regularity, but it need not be restricted to this class.

Miracle, Coincidence, and Counterfactual

I have argued that in order to identify an event as a miracle, we need not show that it is any sense contrary to natural law. Given the occurrence of some extraordinary event E, describing E as a miracle does not commit us to saying that E cannot be subsumed under natural law. Indeed E may be what has been described as a religiously significant coincidence. It is enough that a miracle be extraordinary, in that it runs counter to our reasonable expectations, and that it be identifiable as an instance of divine agency. I have offered *due thankability* as one model for divine agency, and tried to show how this model works to distinguish divine actions in nature without relying on the language of causation.

But now an objection may arise. If E is consistent with natural law, then at least in principle, E might have been predicted by reference to natural forces alone; those forces would be sufficient for its production. But if that is true, then where does God fit into the picture? We want to attribute the event to God's agency, but a reference to divine agency now appears superfluous. The problem is that, in the case of an event having a natural explanation, there seems to be good reason for saying that E would have happened *whether or not* God willed it. And as this might particularly affect the thankability criterion: Why should we thank God for the occurrence of an event that was going to happen anyway? To return to the example of Holland's train: Why should we suppose that God is responsible for the stopping of the train – and why should the child's mother thank God for this – when it was the result of natural forces?

Such concerns have prompted some commentators to insist that a miracle must be an event which would not have happened had God not intervened in the natural world, where this introduces the idea that some supernatural cause is operating. This objection is given by Michael Levine (2002):

A miracle, philosophically speaking, is never a mere coincidence no matter how extraordinary or significant. (If you miss a plane and the plane crashes, that is not a miracle unless God intervened

in the natural course of events causing you to miss the flight.)
A miracle is a supernaturally (divinely) caused event – an event
(ordinarily) different from what would have occurred in the
normal ('natural') course of events. It is a divine overriding of, or
interference with, the natural order.

Suppose that Archibald misses his plane and subsequently the
plane crashes. Levine wants to say that this is not a miracle unless
Archibald missed his plane as a result of God's intervention into the
natural order. Now it is important that we sort out a couple of issues
here.

First, I should point out that given the conception of 'miracle'
that I have developed thus far, I agree with Levine that an event is
not a miracle if it would have occurred in the normal course of
events. Where we differ is in our understanding of what is meant by
'the normal course of events'. Levine thinks that this implies that a
miracle must be an intervention into natural law, and I take it that
he means by this that it is something that would not have occurred
had the laws of nature been operating as they normally do. I want
to argue, as against Levine, that an event may be extraordinary,
running counter to the ordinary or normal course of events, even
if it has a natural explanation. An event is sufficiently extraordinary
to qualify as a miracle if it is something that occurs in the face of
our reasonable expectations to the contrary. This may, of course,
mean that it is contrary to our understanding of natural law, but it
need not mean this. Supposing that Archibald fails to make his
plane because, just before he was ready to get into his car, it was
struck by lightning from a freak storm. This would be sufficient to
capture the fundamental understanding of a miracle as a *wonder*
even if the lightning strike were understood to have occurred as a
result of natural causes.

Second, if what Levine means to say here is that this cannot be
a miracle if its occurrence is consistent with natural law, then he
begs the question against the possibility of coincidence miracles.
But I think we can give a more charitable interpretation of his criticism. He wants to say that a miracle must be 'supernaturally
caused', and if an event has a supernatural cause, then its occur-

rence must be at variance with what *would* have occurred if only natural forces had been operating. Now I have already said quite a lot about the attempt to conceive of a miracle as supernaturally caused. But I think the objection may proceed without this element, though I hesitate to claim that my reconstruction of Levine's argument is in accordance with his intentions. Let us say that Archibald's missing the plane cannot be a miracle unless it is something that would not have occurred had God not *acted* – thus substituting the more general description 'God has acted' for Levine's 'God has intervened in the natural order'.

Thus the objection, as I have reconstructed it, is that we cannot understand Archibald's missing the plane as a miracle unless a counterfactual is satisfied: we must be able to say that Archibald would not have missed the plane had God not intended for him to miss it. Understood in this way, the criticism is really directed against the suggestion that an event can express divine agency if it would have happened regardless of God's intent that it happen, and I wish to suggest that this claim is, in a fairly obvious and straightforward way, true.

Thus I think Levine is right to say that we cannot call an event a miracle, at least in the sense in which that term is used in theistic religion, if it is something that would have happened regardless of God's intentions. If it is a miracle that Archibald missed the plane, then it was God's will that Archibald miss it; Archibald's missing the plane was an action on God's part; Archibald would *not* have missed it were it not for God's intention that he miss it. Of course, as we have already observed, there is a sense in which, if we think that this event shows divine purpose, then it is not really a coincidence at all; we would be thinking of the concatenation of events that led up to Archibald's missing the plane as something that occurred by design. The problem that faces us now is, how can we, without confusion, think of this event as something that happened in accordance with God's intention, if we can account for its occurrence as a result of nothing more than natural forces? Once we see that the event has a natural explanation, what room is left for saying that God's intention was operating in this case? There *is* no room, the critic will say – and it is clear that this is what Levine would like to argue.

I have agreed that the occurrence of a miracle must satisfy a counterfactual; to conceive of some event *E* as a miracle means conceiving of it as being something that would not have occurred were it not for God's intention that it occur. (Let us refer to this as a *counterfactual of agency*.) My concern is to show that *E* may express divine agency, and satisfies the necessary counterfactual, even though it has a natural explanation.

Counterfactuals and Basic Actions

We may find the beginning of our solution to this problem if we consider how counterfactuals of agency are satisfied in the case of human actions. Let us begin by considering a case of non-basic action. Suppose Alfred burns down a house. Since we are conceiving of Alfred's burning down the house as a non-basic action on his part, we are supposing that there is something that Alfred did to *cause* the house to burn down. Let us suppose that he burned down the house by lighting a pile of kerosene-soaked rags. Thus, the house's burning down traces its causal ancestry to something that can be attributed to Alfred's agency, namely, his lighting of the rags. In this case we can assert a counterfactual, saying that the house would not have burned down had Alfred not lit the rags.

On the other hand, if Alfred is not guilty of the arson, he can always make his defense by arguing that the house's burning down can be attributed to some other cause – a *natural* cause, we might say – such as a lightning strike. An alternative causal account makes our reference to Alfred's agency redundant, but only because Alfred's suspected agency in this case would be non-basic.

What about basic actions, then? It is interesting to note that basic actions, too, satisfy a counterfactual. When I raise my hand, a state of affairs occurs – namely, my hand's rising – that would not have occurred were it not for my intention.[3] That is, it seems to be possible to say, in a straightforward way, that if I raised my arm intentionally, then my arm would not have gone up had I not intended to raise it. Yet I cannot be said to have *caused* my hand to go up, at least if this is taken to mean that there is anything that I did in order to bring it about that the hand went up. Nor can I be said to have caused my hand to go up, if the sense of 'cause' that is operating here excludes the possibility that there is a physical cause for its rising. For undoubtedly we can be given a neuro-physiological account for my hand's going up. The truth of such an account, however, does not preclude the possibility of our being able to say that my hand is up *because I intended to raise it.* Thus a counterfactual of agency may be satisfied even though my hand's going up – the event that is what we have referred to as a *companion* to my action in raising my hand – has a physical explanation in terms of neural firings and muscular contractions, etc.

I will recapitulate what we have just said. Suppose that I raise my hand; here I am describing an action on my part. Since I acted in raising my hand, it is correct to say that the companion event – my hand's going up – would not have occurred had I not intended to raise my hand. Thus the counterfactual of agency is satisfied. However, this is compatible with saying that there is a physiological explanation for the occurrence of the companion event in terms of neural firings, etc.

Let us now see how all of this applies to Archibald and the missed plane. We want to say that God makes it the case that Archibald misses the plane; here we are describing a divine action. Since this is a divine action, then it is correct to say that the companion event – the missing of the plane by Archibald – would not have occurred had God not intended for Archibald to miss the plane. Thus the counterfactual of agency is satisfied. Yet, analogous to what we have just observed about my raising my hand, this is compatible with the possibility that the companion event – the missing of the plane by Archibald – has a natural explanation, perhaps to be filled out by reference to the occurrence of a freak weather condition, etc.

In a sense, this observation brings us full circle. One of our earliest observations was that the supernaturalist hopes to see in a miracle an event that would not have occurred were it not for God's agency. Unfortunately, the supernaturalist hopes to make this a matter of a violation of the laws of nature, the intrusion of some supernatural force. But if the argument I have just given is correct, we can accomplish this aim without incurring the weighty baggage of supernaturalism.

I now conclude the present work. I have carefully considered a traditional appeal to miracles, which I have characterized as *supernaturalistic*. The supernaturalist program, as I have outlined it here, is frequently motivated by an apologetic interest, which involves pointing to the occurrence of a miracle as evidence for the existence of a transcendent God. The supernaturalist normally does this by arguing that a miracle is a violation of natural law, and therefore an event that cannot be explained by reference to natural causes; she hopes to invoke supernatural causation – typically, causation by God – as the only explanation available. And of course the chief concern of the supernaturalist is to show that naturalism is incomplete: we cannot account for everything that occurs in nature by reference to natural objects and natural forces; neither is the method of the natural sciences adequate to explain everything that happens in nature.

I have tried to show the problems that come with such a supernaturalistic account. I began by offering a criticism of the idea that an event which fails to be subsumable under natural law must thereby be understood as a violation. I then considered the notion of a supernatural cause, arguing that if we conceive such causes as too similar to natural causes, we have no grounds for calling them supernatural; on the other hand, if they are too different from natural causes, it is hard to see what will justify our referring to them as causes. I have also argued that we cannot conceive of how nature might interact with the supernatural, pointing to the similarity of this problem to the problem of mind–body interaction from which substance dualism suffers.

I have also considered the possibility that we might give specially supernatural explanations for events that might occur in nature. If such explanations are to qualify as adequate under the criteria generally used by the natural sciences, they must be testable, and if they are testable then they are not supernatural explanations, but natural ones. However, I have suggested that we may explain an event by referring it to divine agency, even where this explanation is not testable in any scientific way; the way in which we make such an event intelligible is to bring it into relation with a theistic view of the world, and a theistic religious practice.

I then defended the conception of a miracle as a basic action on the part of God. Such a conception avoids the difficulties that come with a supernaturalist account. One of the most interesting consequences of our thinking of miracles in this way is that we do not have to eliminate the possibility that an event has a natural cause in order to be warranted in referring it to divine agency.

I considered some objections to my account of miracles as basic divine actions. I have argued that the success of such an account does not depend on our saying that the world is God's body. I also considered the objection that an account of divine agency must tell us *how* God acts in the world; some philosophers, pursuing the question of the 'causal joint' between God and natural processes, have sought to locate divine agency at the level of microprocesses such as quantum states. I have tried to show what the limits are to our 'how' questions regarding divine agency, and argued that God may act, in a basic way, at the level of ordinary human experience.

Finally, I have tried to show how we may, within the context of theistic religion – and operating under its assumptions regarding the reality of God and the possibility of God's action in the natural world – identify an event as a miracle. We may do this when we describe an extraordinary event as an instance of divine agency, connecting in some way with the interests of human beings, and mediating a relationship between humanity and the divine. I have also tried to show how a divine action may satisfy a counterfactual – allowing us to say that some event would not have occurred had God not intended it – even though the event in question may have a natural cause.

I hope, therefore, to have accomplished my primary purpose, which has been to show how the concept of 'miracle' may be rescued from the quasi-scientific language of supernaturalism, and given a home in which our discussion of the miraculous proceeds by examining the significance of a miracle for human life and its role in the practice of theistic religion.

Notes

Introduction

1 By a *deterministic regularity* I mean one that may be expressed in terms of a universal generalization of the form 'All As are Bs'. Thus the claim that I wish to make here is the obvious one, which is that there is no logical difficulty in suggesting that an A may occur that is not a B, even though all of the other As have been Bs. Of course the occurrence of such an event seems, fairly obviously, to show that it is not in fact the case that all As are Bs. This issue will be discussed in more detail in Chapter 1.

2 It is possible, however, to defend a supernaturalistic account without resorting to any such conception; see Larmer (1996).

3 It is possible of course that there are close connections among these issues; I would not want to be understood here as suggesting that they may be separated by any sharp lines.

4 For an interesting discussion on this issue see Gealey (2004).

5 I will undertake no commitment as to whether this should be construed as an epistemic or an ontic category. I do want to make clear, however, that it *need* not be epistemic, so that, as our understanding of natural law increases and we become better able to predict what will happen in nature, we become able to predict things that we could not have predicted previously. We can think of extraordinariness as an ontic category as well – for example, there may be events that are indeterminate and can only be predicted statistically; some state of affairs may have a likelihood of occurring only once every million years or so. Our failure to predict its occurrence on a particular occasion would not be the result of our ignorance of the laws of nature and so would not be curable by learning any more. I do not, however, wish to argue that this is how miracles must be.

Chapter 1

1 We should acknowledge that the term 'anomaly' must be used here only with some qualification. An undetermined event would be anomalous – in the sense of failing to be subsumable under any law of nature – only to the extent that the laws of nature are thought of as

deterministic. Thus we might state a law of nature under the form 'All As are Bs', and then speak of an anomaly as an A that is not a B. However, one might argue that the occurrence of such an event would show that the best we can say is that some (very high) percentage of As are Bs. An A that is not a B would not be anomalous in regard to such a statistical law.

2 There are some generalizations, such as 'Objects made of lead will fall when released', that we might be reluctant to conceive in terms of statistical generalizations. More likely we would suppose that the statistical generalization would come at a deeper level of analysis – that gravity involves some element that is subject to statistical generalization.

3 Swinburne makes important use of this assumption in his defense of the teleological argument for the existence of God; see (1992) and particularly p. 138, on which he asserts that 'the universe is characterized by vast, all-pervasive temporal order, the conformity of nature to formula, recorded in the scientific laws formulated by men'. It is hard to see how this claim could be defended if, for any given event, the hypothesis that it conforms to the laws of nature is to receive equal treatment to the idea that it does not.

4 Again, by a *deterministic* law I mean a law having the form of a universal generalization, e.g. 'All As are Bs'. It would still be open to us to say that nature conforms to statistical laws.

5 This would most likely be taken to imply that events of the relevant type are subject to statistical laws. If so, the objection here seems to overlap a point that we have made already, which is that the occurrence of an A that is not a B does not violate a statistical generalization that specifies that some percentage of As will be Bs.

6 Indeed I think that if the naturalist were convinced of the occurrence of some anomaly on the level of ordinary experience, such as the turning of water into wine, his or her first suspicion would likely be that this was the result of some odd concatenation of non-deterministic phenomena occurring at the subatomic level.

Chapter 2

1 Mackie speaks of the possibility that the universe is usually 'closed', as though the supernaturalist wants to claim that it opens to outside influence only occasionally. No doubt many who would defend supernaturalism would claim that supernatural influences operate only occasionally. However, in what follows I will understand the 'open universe' view as holding that the universe is *susceptible* to outside causal influence. Thus as I will speak of the matter, supernaturalism implies that the universe is *always* open to supernatural influence even though such influence may manifest itself only on rare occasions.

2 My use of the expression 'open universe' supernaturalism might be taken as rhetorically suggesting that there may be some other kind. It is true that I would leave open the possibility that supernaturalism might be constructed along different lines. However, in the present context at least, let us simply understand this expression as underscoring the fact that the usual conception of the supernatural subscribes to the view that the natural universe is causally open.

3 Cf. the chapter by this title in Ward's book *Divine Action* (1990).

4 Tracy locates these gaps in quantum indeterminacies, and therefore is not committed to saying that divine agency in an open universe implies any inconsistency with natural law. He also makes clear that divine action is limited to gaps in the causal order of nature. See Tracy (2000: 319).

5 C. S. Lewis (1947: 60ff.).

6 This is Kemp-Smith's summary of her position (Descartes 1952: 273).

Chapter 3

1 Horace Bushnell defends this position (1860).

2 My assumption here is that the presence of teleological elements means that agency is involved. Undoubtedly it is possible to speak of teleology without invoking agency, i.e. without mentioning anyone's will, intentions, or purposes, etc.; in Aristotle, for example, agency is a sufficient but not a necessary condition for *telos*. As I use the term, 'agency' will always indicate an instance of *action*, and, following Davidson, I will say that someone 'is the agent of an act if what he does can be described under an aspect that makes it intentional' (1982: 46). An intentional or *agentive* account therefore becomes a special case of a teleological one. I am, for the most part, concerned here to restrict my consideration of teleological accounts to agentive ones and will not attempt to give any broader construction than this to the notion of teleology. I am, however, open to someone's wanting to construct a broader account, along, for example, Aristotelian lines and I will, in what follows, be concerned to explicitly provide for this possibility from time to time.

3 I think another quite interesting problem arises for the supernaturalist, which is connected with the task of saying what it is about the child's cure that points to a *transcendent* deity rather than one that is immanent in the world, such as the God of the Stoics. The existence of the Stoic God is consistent with the tenets of naturalism. I will not pursue this matter here.

4 See for example Swinburne (1979), as well as Houston (1994). One might also appeal to the principles of historical explanation as being analogous to supernatural explanations. I will not deal separately with

this latter prospect; however, what I have to say here, in regard to personal explanation, will apply with little modification to the suggestion that supernatural explanations are modeled after historical ones.

5   It may be possible to find as many as twelve miracles associated with Elijah, some of which precede the immolation of the bull; see for example the raising of the widow's son at 1 Kings 17.17. Remarkably he is reported to have summoned fire on two occasions; the second is the incineration of the king's soldiers at 2 Kings 1.9.

6   Nowell-Smith points out that there are many kinds of laws, and he includes biological and psychological laws among these (1955: 249). He might, therefore, be happy to call the generalization that we are considering here a law. I will not adopt this terminology.

7   When I speak of an agent as 'non-embodied' I mean simply an agent that has no body. I do not use the expression 'disembodied' because it suggests an agent that was once embodied but is no longer. Disembodied agents, if any exist, would of course be a subset of the non-embodied ones.

8   As far as I can tell, there is no reason why fiction cannot be relevant to determining the meaning of a word. The term 'miracle', for example, does not depend on the truth of any miracle reports.

9   I should make it clear that I have no incentive to defend any definition for 'supernatural'. Still, I might point out that it does not seem correct to limit the supernatural to instances of non-embodied agency. Embodied agents might be capable of expressing their agency in ways that exceed ordinary bodily powers; if Harry can call fire from the sky, this would be an example. We might then say not that Harry is a supernatural agent but that Harry is a natural agent possessing a supernatural power, namely the power to bring fire down from the sky. I am not persuaded that this requires any mention of a violation of natural law; *prima facie*, it seems to be enough that this is something that lies well beyond ordinary human agency, as that is mediated by bodily movements. However, I will not attempt a full investigation of this possibility here.

10 They are of course teleological, which makes them quite different from the sort of explanations that make reference to quarks. But the point is of course that naturalism can, in principle, accommodate the existence of unobservable entities and this seems to be true of entities that are conceived as expressing agency.

11 Some of the miracles in the New Testament appear to involve some sort of prediction. I have in mind the reports of Jesus' healings. The Gospel accounts report that people came, or were brought, to Jesus for healing and this makes little sense if they do not *expect* to be healed. This expectation might have some grounds in the fact that Jesus had

already been reported to work many other healings. However, a good number of the miracles wrought by Jesus seem to be genuinely surprising.

12 There is a scriptural basis for this, e.g. in Romans 10.19, Acts 2.24 and 3.15 (NIV).

13 I can imagine someone wanting to argue that some sort of eschatological predictions are possible here. I am inclined to think that this only serves to bring up a whole new set of problems. In any case, my point is that we are not *obliged* to make any appeal to the possibility of making such predictions.

Chapter 4

1 See for example Mumford (2001).

2 I mean of course to exclude the more ordinary sense of 'miracle' by which one may refer to the miracle of birth, etc.

3 See for example the *Acchariya-abbhuta Sutta* in the Majjhima Nikaya (Nanamoli and Bodhi 1995: 979).

4 Bushnell seems to want to draw a very close analogy between divine and human basic actions, referring to both as 'supernatural'. Bushnell's account is highly interesting and I regret that I cannot discuss it in detail here.

5 Goldman (1976: 24) makes this point using a different example.

6 I may not have intended to alert the prowler; nevertheless, on Davidson's view, it is an action on my part because I intended to move my fingers in the way I did.

7 It is worth noting that even if we did have some idea of what sort of natural process might account for the turning of water into wine – perhaps some combination of physically possible, though statistically improbable, quantum phenomena – we would still have the task of explaining how God could initiate such a process. Assuming that we wish to think of this initiation in terms of causation, we are thrown onto the other horn of the dilemma, which is the task of explaining how a causal interaction is possible between nature and the supernatural.

8 A complication arises in the case of human agency, which is that the nature of the neurological processes involved in the rising of someone's arm are not irrelevant to the question of her agency. We might find, on close examination of her brain, that she is in the midst of a seizure, and this will give us good reason to doubt whether she really is (intentionally) raising her hand, or whether her hand is merely rising in an involuntary way. At the very least, there may be neurological states that are incompatible with the proposition that an agent's arm movement is voluntary, so that the presence of such states

becomes a defeater for the proposition that she is raising her arm, i.e. that she is acting. As far as I know, there are no neurological criteria by which we can determine, positively, that someone is intentionally moving her arm, but for all I know, someday there will be. Thus there may be internal neurological criteria for determining whether someone is engaged in voluntary activity. Such criteria would complement the external criteria that are supplied by asking whether her arm movement is consistent with our understanding of her character and what we know of her purposes. We might for example suspect that her arm movement is involuntary if it has a result that is inconsistent with her interests, e.g. it results in her successfully bidding at auction for a painting she is known to dislike and which she cannot afford.

I think what we ought to say about this kind of case is that it represents a disanalogy between human and divine agency. Because there does not seem to be anything that corresponds to a divine neurological state, the only criteria we seem to have at our disposal, in trying to determine whether an event in nature may be associated with divine agency, is whether it is consistent with what we know of God's purposes; that is, the only criteria available to us are external ones. In any case, the point I want to make here is that the fact that it is possible to give a physical explanation for the rising of someone's arm is not, in principle, incompatible with saying that she is performing a basic action in raising her arm.

9 One may be inclined to suppose that there are other things God does in order to bring Jesus back to life, e.g. first starting his heart, etc. Such an inclination may come from the recognition that the returning to life of a dead man would be a very complex physiological occurrence. But of course, while the raising of my arm is surely not nearly such a complex phenomenon, it is still the case that my intention to raise it has no regard for this complexity. Thus there is no reason to restrict basic actions to simple phenomena. I do not see why Jesus cannot come back to life as a direct result (so to speak) of God's intention that he do so, regardless of how complex the process of coming back to life might be. (If we want to avoid speaking of this as a *result*, which may be seen as carrying causal connotations, we might refer to Jesus' resurrection as the *direct expression* of God's intention that he come back to life.)

Chapter 5

1 The point here also seems relevant to the debate on how divine agency may be reconciled with evolutionary processes. I cannot, of course, pursue this issue here.

2 I am following Hornsby here; see (1980: 70).

3 The context of Saunders's description is his attack on Grace Jantzen's view that God's actions in the world are basic; that is, it is clear that Saunders is critical of the suggestion that God should act in such a manner.

4 To say that they *may* be relevant is to invite the speculation that they *may not* be. In respect of a non-basic divine action, the search for a mechanism does not involve any conceptual confusion, as it does in the case of a basic action. Nevertheless there is no guarantee that the answer will be *theologically* interesting.

5 If God parts the Red Sea as a non-basic action, then the raising of the wind must be sufficient to bring it about that the waters part in the way Exodus describes this happening. I do not pretend to know how this might be possible, and if it is not, then we might want to say that the parting of the waters was itself a basic divine action. I will not trouble over the details here, and propose to treat this as a case of non-basic action. What interests me is the conceptual issue – that God is represented as parting the Red Sea by doing something else.

6 Once again this is to accept as unproblematic my understanding of the Exodus account, which describes God as parting the Red Sea by raising the east wind. I can imagine someone wanting to argue that a strong wind is not sufficient to account for the parting of the Red Sea as Exodus describes it, and certainly will not account for how the waters could remain parted while the Israelites walk through. In this case there might be an additional action, to be described as God's holding back the water, which might be basic as well. I do not think these complications affect the conclusion I wish to draw here.

7 As I hope I have made clear, I am not particularly concerned to argue that God's actions are consistent with physical theory; I have no objection to anyone who claims that some of the events that God brings about are anomalies, i.e. that they are not instances of any natural law. Nevertheless, since I have argued that it doesn't matter, I must be able to say that an event's being subsumable under natural law doesn't *prevent* us from associating it with divine agency.

8 One alternative to such an approach is to say that God performs a 'master act' in creating the physical universe together with its system of laws, and that subsequent details in the way that the universe unfolds may be counted as 'sub-acts'. Gordon Kaufman is particularly associated with this view; see Chapter 6 of his *God the Problem* (1972). I cannot consider detailed objections to Kaufman's view here. However, an obvious problem will be with how it can avoid the charge that it does not understand God as actively involved with the world. Such an involvement is generally presumed by theism (as opposed to deism) and seems to be presupposed by theistic religious practices such as petitionary prayer.

9 In a footnote Van Inwagen explains that he does want to say that, once Y comes into existence, God's sustaining the world implies that God must issue countless decrees aimed at sustaining the existence of the elementary particles that constitute Y, together with their causal powers (1988: 227n). I do not see why this should be true. If God cannot bring about Y, composed as it is of innumerable particles, with the general decree 'Let there be either X or Y', then I do not see why God could not sustain those particles with the general decree 'Let Y endure'.

10 I would certainly allow that it is possible that on some occasions, God might engage in micromanagement. What concerns me is the assumption that this is how God normally works in the world. By contrast I want to argue here for the opposite presumption, which I take to be rebuttable, which is that God acts at the macro level of ordinary human experience.

11 Compton acknowledges his indebtedness to Kaufman (1972: 39) and so may not be deeply concerned about providing for special divine agency.

12 One may argue that in such a case, God may intervene into the natural order; however, it seems to me that once God has done that, it is no longer correct to say that the physical universe is deterministic, since at least one event will have occurred that was not determined by antecedent physical conditions.

13 Phillip Clayton observes that alternative models of human agency may hold more promise; see 1997: 212.

14 It could be that a physical analysis of the event would turn up the fact that it is due to a seizure of some kind, which would rule out the possibility of saying that she has (intentionally) raised her hand. It would be wrong, therefore, to say that such an inquiry could never be relevant. However, in the ordinary case – and particularly so long as the action coheres with our understanding of the agent's character and purposes – the physiological question would not come up. This means that understanding that she has acted, in raising her hand, *need* not require any inquiry into the mechanism of her hand's rising; that is, as I have said here, it is not a general requirement. It would seem to follow that such an inquiry *need* not be required in the case of divine action; indeed, given that there seems to be no equivalent, in the case of divine action, to this sort of neurological dysfunction, it is hard to see how it could *ever* arise. Questions about whether God has acted will always be connected, not with any inquiry into a physical mechanism, but with the issue of whether the putative action is consistent with our understanding of God's character and purposes.

Chapter 6

1 Of course from another perspective it is no coincidence at all, i.e. if we see the stopping of the train as an action on God's part; thinking of it in this way involves seeing a connection between these two events. Seen in this way the stopping of the train is something that happens for a reason.

2 There is much that might be said regarding just what sort of needs might be involved here. I can imagine someone wanting to argue that divine agency ought to be associated only with needs that are shared among all human beings, and particularly with those that are felt the most deeply. This would rule out the possibility of finding divine agency in the satisfaction of trivial needs: 'Thank God I made that traffic signal! I might have been late for my appointment.' I have no particular objection to enlarging the sphere of divine agency to encompass such relatively trivial needs, and I do not think it is at odds with theistic religious practice to suppose that God is involved, more or less continuously, in our lives, even when the stakes are not particularly large. We might want to allow, however, that the really important instances of divine agency are those that are properly associated with our deepest needs, and my intuition is that miracles should be restricted to this category. However, I will not try to settle any of these issues here.

3 This is the usual case; I do not mean to deny that there may be cases in which the raising of my arm is overdetermined by the fact that there is someone waiting to raise it for me, should I fail to raise it on my own. I am satisfied to show that a counterfactual of agency *can* be satisfied in the presence of a physical explanation for a given bodily movement.

Bibliography

Alston, William P. (1994), 'Divine Action: Shadow or Substance', in Thomas
F. Tracy (ed.), *The God Who Acts* (University Park: Pennsylvania State
University Press).

Aquinas, Thomas (1905), *Summa Contra Gentiles*, trans. Joseph Rickaby, in
Of God and His Creatures (London: Burns & Oates).

Bushnell, Horace (1860), *Nature and the Supernatural* (New York: C. Scribner).

Clarke, Steve (2003), 'Response to Mumford and another Definition of
Miracles', *Religious Studies* 39: 459–63.

Clayton, Phillip D. (1997), *God and Contemporary Science* (Edinburgh: Edinburgh University Press).

Compton, John (1972), 'Science and God's Action in Nature', in Ian G.
Barbour (ed.), *Earth Might Be Fair: Reflections on Ethics, Religion, and
Ecology* (Englewoods Cliffs: Prentice-Hall).

Danto, Arthur C. (1965), 'Basic Actions', *American Philosophical Quarterly* 2:
141–48.

— (1968), 'Basic Actions', in Alan R. White (ed.), *The Philosophy of Action*
(Oxford: Oxford University Press).

Davidson, Donald (1982), *Essays on Action and Events* (New York: Oxford
University Press).

Descartes, Rene (1952), *Descartes' Philosophical Writings*, trans. Norman Kemp
Smith (London: Macmillan).

Dietl, Paul (1968), 'On Miracles', *American Philosophical Quarterly* 5: 130–34.

Dubbs, Homer (1950), 'Miracles – A Contemporary Attitude', *Hibbert Journal*
48 (January): 159–62.

Farrer, Austin (1967), *Theology and Speculation* (London: A. and C. Black).

Flew, Anthony (1966), *God and Philosophy* (New York: Harcourt, Brace and
World).

— (1967), 'Miracles', in *Encyclopedia of Philosophy* (New York: Macmillan and
Free Press), vol. 5, 346–53.

— (1984), *God: A Critical Enquiry* (La Salle: Open Court Publishing).

— (1997), *Hume's Philosophy of Belief* (Bristol: Thoemmes Press).

Gealy, Walford (2004), 'Is There An Audience for Miracles?' in D. Z. Phillips
and Mario von der Ruhr (eds), *Biblical Concepts and Our World* (New
York: Palgrave Macmillan).

Geivett, R. Douglas (1997), 'The Evidential Value of Miracles', in R. Douglas Geivett and Gary R. Habermas (eds), *In Defense of Miracles: A Comprehensive Case for God's Action in History* (Downers Grove: Intervarsity Press).

Goldman, Alvin I. (1976), *A Theory of Human Action* (Princeton: Princeton University Press).

Hartshorne, Charles (1983), *Omnipotence and Other Theological Mistakes* (Albany: State University of New York Press).

Hick, John (1973), *God and the Universe of Faiths* (Oxford: Oneworld Publications).

Holland, R. F. (1965), 'The Miraculous', *American Philosophical Quarterly* 2: 43–51.

— (1989), 'Lusus Naturae', in D. Z. Phillips and Peter Winch (eds), *Wittgenstein: Attention to Particulars* (New York: St. Martin's Press).

Hornsby, Jennifer (1980), *Actions* (London: Routledge & Kegan Paul).

Houston, J. (1994), *Reported Miracles* (Cambridge: Cambridge University Press).

Hume, David (1975), *Enquiries Concerning Human Understanding*, ed. L. A. Selby-Bigge (Oxford: Oxford University Press).

Huxley, T. H. (1894), *Collected Essays. Vol. VI. Hume: With Helps to the Study of Berkeley* (New York: D. Appleton and Co.).

Jantzen, Grace (1984), *God's World, God's Body* (Philadelphia: Westminster Press).

Kaufman, Gordon D. (1972), *God the Problem* (Cambridge: Harvard University Press).

Kellenberger, J. (1979), 'Miracles', *International Journal for Philosophy of Religion* 10: 145–62.

Larmer, Robert (1996), *Water into Wine: An Investigation of the Concept of Miracle* (Montreal: McGill-Queen's University Press).

Lewis, C. S. (1947), *Miracles* (New York: Macmillan).

Levine, Michael P. (1989), *Hume and the Problem of Miracles: A Solution* (Dordrecht: Kluwer Publishers).

— (2002), 'Miracles', in *The Stanford Encyclopedia of Philosophy* (Winter 2002), ed. Edward N. Zalta, http://plato.stanford.edu/archives/win2002/entries/miracles.

Lunn, Arnold (1950), 'Miracles – The Scientific Approach', *Hibbert Journal* 48 (April): 240–46.

Mackie, J. L. (1982), *The Miracle of Theism* (Oxford: Oxford University Press).

Macmurray, John (1991), *The Self as Agent* (Amherst: Humanity Books).

Mavrodes, George I. (1985), 'Miracles and the Laws of Nature', *Faith and Philosophy* 2.4 (October): 333–46.

McFague, Sally (1993), *The Body of God: An Ecological Theology* (Minneapolis: Fortress Press).

McKinnon, Alastair (1967). '"Miracle" and "Paradox"', *American Philosophical Quarterly* 4: 308–14.

Melden, A. I. (1961), *Free Action* (London: Routledge & Kegan Paul).

Mumford, Stephen (2001), 'Miracles: Metaphysics and Modality', *Religious Studies* 37: 191–202.

Nanamoli and Bodhi, trans. (1995), *The Middle Length Discourses of the Buddha* (Somerville: Wisdom Publications).

Nowell-Smith, Patrick (1955), 'Miracles', in Antony Flew and Alasdair MacIntyre (eds), *New Essays in Philosophical Theology* (New York: Macmillan).

Ott, Ludwig (1955), *Fundamentals of Catholic Dogma*, trans. Patrick Lynch (Rockford: Tan Books and Publishers Inc.).

Penelhum, Terence (1970), *Survival and Non-embodied Existence* (London: Routledge & Kegan Paul).

Phillips, D. Z. (1999), *Recovering Religious Concepts* (New York: St. Martin's Press).

Polkinghorne, John (2003), *Belief in God in an Age of Science* (New Haven: Yale University Press).

Saunders, Nicholas (2002), *Divine Action and Modern Science* (Cambridge: Cambridge University Press).

Smart, Ninian (1964), *Philosophers and Religious Truth* (New York: Macmillan).

Swinburne, Richard (1970), *The Concept of Miracle* (London: Macmillan).

— (1992), *The Existence of God* (Oxford: Clarendon Press [1979]).

Taylor, Richard (1966), *Action and Purpose* (Englewoods Cliffs: Prentice-Hall Inc.).

Tracy, Thomas F. (2000), 'Particular Providence and the God of the Gaps', in R. Russell, N. Murphy and A. Peacocke (eds), *Chaos and Complexity: Scientific Perspectives on Divine Action* (The Vatican: Vatican Observatory; Berkeley: Center for Theology and the Natural Sciences).

Van Inwagen, Peter (1988), 'Chance in a World Sustained by God', in Thomas V. Morris (ed.), *Divine and Human Action: Essays in the Metaphysics of Theism* (Ithaca: Cornell University Press).

Ward, Keith (1990), *Divine Action* (London: Collins).

White, Vernon (1985), *The Fall of a Sparrow* (Exeter: Paternoster Press).

Winch, Peter (1995), 'Asking Too Many Questions', in Timothy Tessin and Mario von der Ruhr (eds), *Philosophy and the Grammar of Religious Belief* (New York: St. Martin's Press).

Wittgenstein, Ludwig (1968), *Philosophical Investigations*, 3rd edn, ed. G. E. M. Anscombe and R. Rhees, trans. G. E. M. Anscombe (New York: Macmillan).

— (1980), *Culture and Value*, trans. Peter Winch (Chicago: University of Chicago Press).

Index

Acchariya-abbuta Sutra   151
Act description   104
Acts, Book of   151
Alienation of God and humanity   76
Alston, William   45
Anomaly   23, 28, 35, 40, 41, 72 and
   passim
Anthropomorphic representation of
   God   63
Anvil   60–1
Aquarium, nature compared to
   46–8
Aquinas   9
Aristotle   8, 149

Basic action   3, 81, 83 and *passim*
Boojums   60, 66, 67
Buddha   82
Bull, immolation of   68, 150
Bushnell, Horace   84, 149

Causal joint   4, 95, 105, 106, 109,
   118, 145
Causal openness of the world   44,
   45, 121, 124
Cause, supernatural; see *supernatural
   cause*
Chaos theory   111
Civil law   19–20
Clarke, Steve   11
Clayton, Phillip   154
Coincidence miracle   129, 131,
   139–41
Companion event   90, 114, 143

Compatibilism   121
Compton, John   119–21, 124, 125,
   154
Contextual conception of the mirac-
   ulous   6, 11, 129, 132
Contingency miracle; see *coincidence
   miracle*
Corinthians II   62
Counterfactual and miracle   129,
   130, 141, 142
Counterfactual of agency   142
Creation of matter   96

Danto, Arthur   84, 85, 98
Davidson, Donald   84–6, 149, 151
Descartes, René   50, 51
Determinism   120
Dietl, Paul   54, 67–74, 77–8
Disease, divine cure   117, 124, 150
Disembodied agency   150
Dualism   42, 43, 49
Dubbs, Homer   57, 58

Edinburgh   106
Egyptians   110, 117
Electrons   61, 62
Elijah   68, 70–5, 80, 150
Elisha   75
Elizabeth, Princess   50, 51
Epistemic conception of the extra-
   ordinary   15
Eschatological prediction   151
Event causation and basic action
   86, 87

Event description 104
Exodus, Book of 109, 110, 115, 153
Experiencing-as 13
Experimental design and miracles 68
Explanation, supernatural; see supernatural explanation
Extraordinary, requirement for the miraculous 14–16

Farrer, Austin 109
Final cause 8
Flew, Antony 2, 18, 19, 21, 25, 32, 35, 36
Free will 122

Gaps, God of the 91
Gaps in the natural order 95, 111, 119, 120
Geivett, R. Douglas 61
Gesture, miracle as 12, 133
Glacier 10
Glasgow 106
God's body 3, 95, 125, 145
Goldman, Alvin 84, 85, 151

Hartshorne, Charles 96
Hick, John 13
Holland, R. F. 4, 12, 128, 130, 131, 134, 136
Hornsby, Jennifer 84, 85, 152
Houston, J. 149
Hume, David 5, 10, 18
Huxley, T. H. 19

Identifying Miracles, Problem of 32
Imagination 98
Infinite regress 86, 87, 108–9, 111
Intentional account of divine action 106
Interaction, mind–body 42, 50
Interaction, nature and supernatural 43, 48, 49, 52, 79, 83, 88–90, 94, 112, 118
Israelites 101, 109, 110, 117

Jantzen, Grace 96, 152
John, Book of 62

Kaufman, Gordon 121, 153, 154
Kellenberger, J. 4, 128, 130, 134–6, 138
Kings I, Book of 68, 150
Kings II, Book of 150

Lancaster, dynasty of 131
Larmer, Robert 9, 45
Leverrier, Urbain 58
Levine, Michael 18, 31, 32, 41, 139–42
Lewis, C. S. 9, 46, 47, 51
Logos 96
Lottery 101–5
Lunn, Arnold 57–60, 63, 69

Mackie, J. L. 44, 45, 148
Macmurray, John 106
Magnet 60
Magnetic field 62
Master act 153
Mavrodes, George 20
McFague, Sally 97
McKinnon, Alastair 2, 17, 19–21, 28, 30
Mechanism for natural–supernatural interaction 47, 72
Melden, A. I. 84
Mental acts as basic 98
Microprocesses 113
Mind–body interaction 2, 50–1
Ming Dynasty 131
Moses 75, 80, 110
Mount Carmel 70
Multiple realizability of divine intentions 114, 116

Mumford, Stephen 11, 151
Murphey, Nancey 111
Muscular contractions and human
    action 90 and *passim*
Mystery and miracle 91

Naturalism, methodological, defined
    6
Naturalism, ontological, defined 6
Neptune 58
Neural states and human agency
    90, 151–2 and *passim*
Nomic agnosticism 81
Nonrepeatable counterinstance to
    natural law 17, 22–30
Nowell-Smith, Patrick 54–6, 63, 66,
    69–74, 77, 150

Occasionalism 50
Ockham's Razor 91, 115
Olympic athlete 11
Ontic conception of the extra-
    ordinary 15–16
Open universe 44–6, 145
Open-door epistemology 92
Orphanage 101–3
Ott, Ludwig 63

Panpsychism 98
Penelhum, Terence 99
Personal Explanation 69, 99–100
Phillips, D. Z. 92
Plato 96
Pneuma 62
Polkinghorne, John 97, 106
Practice, religious 117
Praise 118
Prayer 117, 118, 153
Predictability and agency 64–6
Predictive expansion 55, 63, 70–1,
    74, 77
Primitive actions 85
Prowler 85, 151

Psychokinesis 98–101, 125; see also
    telekinesis

Quantum states 95, 111, 113–17,
    122, 123, 124, 149
Quarks 61–2, 150

Ramanuja 96
Random process 101–3
Reconciliation of God with humanity
    76
Red Sea, parting of 101, 109–11,
    113, 116, 153
Resurrection of Jesus 76, 92, 93,
    152
Romans, Book of 151
Russell, Robert John 111

Sapple 36–7
Saunders, Nicholas 87, 88, 106,
    107, 109, 129, 135, 136, 152
Simplicity of God 62
Smart, Ninian 17, 20, 23–30, 40
Special divine agency 106, 115,
    119–21, 123–5
Statistical law 148
Stoics 96, 149
Sub-acts of God's master act 153
Subatomic particles 91, 115
Substance dualism 2, 42, 50
Superfluous, reference to divine
    agency as 139
Supernatural cause 1, 2, 6, 17,
    31–9, 41–2 and *passim*
Supernatural explanation 2, 7, 18,
    28 and *passim*
Supernatural force 2, 10, 18, 21,
    30–4, 77, 80, 104
Supernatural power 9, 79, 150
Supernaturalism, causal 1
Supernaturalistic conception of the
    miraculous 6–10
Super-scientist, God as 92

Supervenience of divine action on microprocesses 105, 113, 116–19, 124
Swinburne, Richard 23, 25–7, 30, 96, 97, 99, 100, 149
Symbolic significance of a miracle 133

Taylor, Richard 64, 65
Telekinesis 82, 99; see also *psychokinesis*
Teleological causes 8, 87
Teleological conception of the miraculous 6, 10–11, 78, 81, 101
Telos 149
Thankability 4, 128–38
Thanksgiving 118
Timaeus 96
Tracy, Thomas 46, 111, 120–5

Train, Holland's 130, 134, 136, 137, 139, 154–5
Trans-domain laws 48

Uniformity of nature, not implied by naturalism 7
Uranus 58

Vaishnava tradition 96
Van Inwagen, Peter 114, 116, 153
Vatican 75

Ward, Keith 45, 149
Water turned into wine 88–90, 105, 151
White, Vernon 99
Winch, Peter 12
Wittgenstein, Ludwig 11–12, 84, 133
Wonder, miracle as 11, 91, 140